The People of China

Shu Shin Luh

Mason Crest
Philadelphia

CHINa
THE EMERGING SUPERPOWER

The People of China

Shu Shin Luh

 Mason Crest
Philadelphia

Mason Crest
370 Reed Road
Broomall, PA 19008
www.masoncrest.com

Copyright © 2013 by Mason Crest, an imprint of National Highlights, Inc.
Printed and bound in the United States of America.

CPSIA Compliance Information: Batch #CH2013-10.
For further information, contact Mason Crest at 1-866-MCP-Book.

First printing

1 3 5 7 9 8 6 4 2

Library of Congress Cataloging-in-Publication Data

Luh, Shu Shin.
 The people of China / Shu Shin Luh.
     p. cm. — (China: the emerging superpower)
 Includes bibliographical references and index.
 ISBN 978-1-4222-2163-1 (hardcover)
 ISBN 978-1-4222-2174-7 (pbk.)
 ISBN 978-1-4222-9452-9 (ebook)
 1. China—Biography—Juvenile literature. I. Title.
 DS706.L84 2012
 305.800951—dc22
                            2010047750

Table of Contents

Introduction

Dr. Jianwei Wang
University of Wisconsin–Stevens Point

Before his first official visit to the United States in December 2003, Chinese premier Wen Jiabao granted a lengthy interview to the *Washington Post*. In that interview, he observed: "If I can speak very honestly and in a straightforward manner, I would say the understanding of China by some Americans is not as good as the Chinese people's understanding of the United States." Needless to say, Mr. Wen was making a sweeping generalization. From my personal experience and observation, some Americans understand China at least as well as some Chinese understand the United States. But overall there remains some truth in Mr. Wen's remarks. For example, if you visited a typical high school in China, you would probably find that students there know more about the United States than their American counterparts know about China. For one thing, most Chinese teenagers start learning English in high school, while only a very small fraction of American high school students will learn Chinese.

In a sense, the knowledge gap between Americans and Chinese about each other is understandable. For the Chinese, the United States is the most important foreign country, representing not just the most developed economy, unrivaled military might, and the most advanced science and technology, but also a very attractive political and value system, which many Chinese admire. But for Americans, China is merely one of many foreign countries. As citizens of the world's sole superpower, Americans naturally feel less compelled to learn from others. The Communist nature of the Chinese polity also gives many Americans pause. This gap of interest in and motivation to learn about the other side could be easily detected by the mere fact that every year tens of thousands of Chinese young men and women apply for a visa to study in the United States. Many of them decide to stay in this country. In comparison, many fewer Americans want to study in China, let alone live in that remote land.

Nevertheless, for better or worse, China is becoming more and more important to the United States, not just politically and economically, but also culturally. Most notably, the size of the Chinese population in the United States has increased steadily. China-made goods as well as Chinese food have become a part of most Americans' daily life. China is now the second-largest trade partner of the United States and will be a huge market for American goods and services. China is also one of the largest creditors, with about $1 trillion in U.S. government securities. Internationally China could either help or hinder American foreign policy in the United Nations, on issues ranging from North Korea to non-proliferation of weapons of mass destruction. In the last century, misperception of this vast country cost the United States dearly in the Korean War and the Vietnam War. On the issue of Taiwan, China and the United States may once again embark on a collision course if both sides are not careful in handling the dispute. Simply put, the state of U.S.-China relations may well shape the future not just for Americans and Chinese, but for the world at large as well.

The purpose of this series, therefore, is to help high school students form an accurate, comprehensive, and balanced understanding of China, past and present, good and bad, success and failure, potential and limit, and culture and state. At least three major images will emerge from various volumes in this series.

First is the image of traditional China. China has the longest continuous civilization in the world. Thousands of years of history produced a rich and sophisticated cultural heritage that still influences today's China. While this ancient civilization is admired and appreciated by many Chinese as well as foreigners, it can also be heavy baggage that makes progress in China difficult and often very costly. This could partially explain why China, once the most advanced country in the world, fell behind during modern times. Foreign encroachment and domestic trouble often plunged this ancient nation into turmoil and war. National rejuvenation and restoration of the historical greatness is still considered the most important mission for the Chinese people today.

Second is the image of Mao's China. The establishment of the People's Republic of China in 1949 marked a new era in this war-torn land. Initially the Communist regime was quite popular and achieved significant accomplishments by bringing order and stability back to Chinese society. When Mao declared that the "Chinese people stood up" at Tiananmen Square, "the sick man of East Asia" indeed reemerged on the world stage as a united and independent power. Unfortunately, Mao soon plunged the country into endless political campaigns that climaxed in the disastrous Cultural Revolution. China slipped further into political suppression, diplomatic isolation, economic backwardness, and cultural stagnation.

Third is the image of China under reform. Mao's era came to an abrupt end after his death in 1976. Guided by Deng Xiaoping's farsighted and courageous policy of reform and openness, China has experienced earth-shaking changes in the last quarter century. With the adoption of a market economy, in just two decades China transformed itself into a global economic powerhouse. China has also become a full-fledged member of the international community, as exemplified by its return to the United Nations and its accession to the World Trade Organization. Although China is far from being democratic as measured by Western standards, overall it is now a more humane place to live, and the Chinese people have begun to enjoy unprecedented freedom in a wide range of social domains.

These three images of China, strikingly different, are closely related with one another. A more sophisticated and balanced perception of China needs to take into consideration all three images and the process of their evolution from one to another, thus acknowledging the great progress China has made while being fully aware that it still has a long way to go. In my daily contact with Americans, I quite often find that their views of China are based on the image of traditional China and of China under Mao—they either discount or are unaware of the dramatic changes that have taken place. Hopefully this series will allow its readers to observe the following realities about China.

First, China is not black and white, but rather—like the United States—complex and full of contradictions. For such a vast country, one or two negative stories in the media often do not represent the whole picture. Surely the economic reforms have reduced many old problems, but they have also created many new problems. Not all of these problems, however, necessarily prove the guilt of the Communist system. Rather, they may be the result of the very reforms the government has been implementing and of the painful transition from one system to another. Those who would view China through a single lens will never fully grasp the complexity of that country.

Second, China is not static. Changes are taking place in China every day. Anyone who lived through Mao's period can attest to how big the changes have been. Every time I return to China, I discover something new. Some things have changed for the better, others for the worse. The point I want to make is that today's China is a very dynamic society. But the development in China has its own pace and logic. The momentum of changes comes largely from within rather than from without. Americans can facilitate but not dictate such changes.

Third, China is neither a paradise nor a hell. Economically China is still a developing country with a very low per capita GDP because of its huge population. As the Chinese premier put it, China may take another 100 years to catch up with the United States. China's political system remains authoritarian and can be repressive and arbitrary. Chinese people still do not have as much freedom as American people enjoy, particularly when it comes to expressing opposition to the government. So China is certainly not an ideal society, as its leaders used to believe (or at least declare). Yet the Chinese people as a whole are much better off today than they were 25 years ago, both economically and politically. Chinese authorities were fond of telling the Chinese people that Americans lived in an abyss of misery. Now every Chinese knows that this is nonsense. It is equally ridiculous to think of the Chinese in a similar way.

Finally, China is both different from and similar to the United States. It is true that the two countries differ greatly in terms of political and social systems and cultural tradition. But it is also true that China's program of reform and openness has made these two societies much more similar. China is largely imitating the United States in many aspects. One can easily detect the convergence of the two societies in terms of popular culture, values, and lifestyle by walking on the streets of Chinese cities like Shanghai. With ever-growing economic and other functional interactions, the two countries have also become increasingly interdependent. That said, it is naïve to expect that China will become another United States. Even if China becomes a democracy one day, these two great nations may still not see eye to eye on many issues.

Understanding an ancient civilization and a gigantic country such as China is always a challenge. If this series kindles readers' interest in China and provides them with systematic information and thoughtful perspectives, thus assisting their formation of an informed and realistic image of this fascinating country, I am sure the authors of this series will feel much rewarded.

Pedestrians walk through a crowded street in Hong Kong. Although nearly 92 percent of China's 1.35 billion people are members of a single ethnic group, the Han, the Chinese government officially recognizes 55 other ethnicities.

Ethnic Diversity and the Chinese Identity

The world's most populous nation, China is home to approximately 1.35 billion people. The overwhelming majority of these people—nearly 92 percent—come from a single ethnic group, the Han. It was principally the Han who shaped Chinese civilization over the course of more than two millennia. But that does not mean that China is a homogeneous country, or that groups other than the Han have not contributed in significant ways to its culture. Indeed, the Han are but one of 56 distinct ethnic groups recognized by the government of China. Traditionally nomadic Mongols, for example, occupy the vast grasslands of northern China, near the Russian border. The Manchus, who share a similar ancestry with the Koreans, came originally from the northeast. The rugged mountains of southwestern China are the home of the Yao and Miao peoples. Tibetans populate "the Rooftop of the World," as the area around the Himalayas is sometimes called. The largely barren far west contains Turkic-speaking Muslims.

In size, China's ethnic minorities vary widely. The largest classified minority, the Zhuang, claims more than 16 million individuals, most of them residing in the Guangxi Zhuang Autonomous Region of the southwest. The smallest, a farming and hunting tribe of Tibet known as the Lhoba, numbers just 3,000. Nine of China's 56 recognized ethnicities can be counted as major groups, based on the size of their population as well as their cultural and political importance. In addition to the Han and the Zhuang, they are the Manchus, Mongols, Tibetans, Hui, Uighurs (also frequently spelled Uygurs), Miao, and Yao. The last of these groups is the smallest; there are about 2.6 million Yao in China. (Population figures in this book are based on China's 2000 census.)

Constructing Identities in China

China is a vast land, roughly the size of the United States, and throughout history it has been the home of a multitude of peoples. Vast migratory movements, as well as the genesis, decline, and fusion of diverse groups, have shaped China's ethnic makeup.

The dominant Han Chinese were themselves a product of the intermixing of many tribes on territory that now makes up China. But even from early times the Han, whose society was founded on agriculture, regarded the nomadic peoples around them with contempt; in the Han view, these peoples were "barbarians." Over the centuries, the non-Han peoples who inhabited central China were pushed inexorably into the borderlands. But under Confucianism, the ideology of the state from the late 3rd century B.C. to the early 20th century A.D., nonviolent assimilation through education and indoctrination in Han Chinese values, rather than extermination, was the preferred option for dealing with minority peoples. The

Three young women, members of the Bouyei ethnic minority, pose in the window of a teahouse in the village of Zheng Shan, Guizhou Province. The Bouyei, who today number almost 3 million, are known for their skill at crafts and for their rich tradition of folk literature.

underlying goal of policy was to maintain the geographic unity of the nation. To do so inevitably entailed both appeasing minority groups and oppressing them—all in the name of creating an over-arching and unifying "Chinese" identity.

When it comes to defining ethnic identity in modern China, poli-tics has weighed heavily. In the 20th century, government policies on minorities have varied greatly, producing markedly different effects on the minorities themselves.

The Nationalist government in the 1920s recognized essentially five nationalities in China: the Han, Tibetans, Manchus, Mongols, and Hui (or Muslims). These categories took no account of the numerous peoples of southern China, such as the Miao, the Bai, and the Zhuang, or of some of those of the north (for example, the Koreans of Yanbian in Jilin Province). Although the Nationalists were staunchly anti-Communist, their minority policies were great-ly influenced by, and often closely mirrored, those of the Soviet

Union. Specifically, the Nationalist government tended to accept notions of self-determination and autonomy for China's minorities. (In the Soviet Union, ethnically based republics had the right—in theory if not in fact—to secede should they so desire.)

But by the mid-1930s, China's Nationalist government feared that allowing self-determination would threaten the larger goal of creating a unified Chinese identity, which the government regarded as essential in the struggle for a modern China. In practice, however, the government was unable to implement its central ideas on Chinese unity and minority groups because widespread corruption, a protracted war with Japan, and economic disintegration exhausted and paralyzed the Nationalist regime in the 1930s and 1940s. During that time, Tibet behaved very much like an independent state, even though it was not recognized as such either by China or by the international community. Manchuria, the region in northeastern China where the Japanese set up the puppet state of Manchukuo in 1932, contained a substantial population of China's minorities, including almost all the Koreans, a high proportion of the Manchus (from which the name Manchuria came), and some of the Mongols.

China's central government long considered Xinjiang, in the extreme northwest, to be part of the country, but before 1949 the control exercised there by central authorities was more theoretical than actual. Xinjiang's proximity to Russia made it a natural satellite subject to control by the Soviet Communists.

By 1931 the Chinese Communist Party (CCP)—though not yet in power—articulated a policy of allowing the secession of minorities that chose to break away from China. This policy went unrealized and was ultimately reversed by Mao Zedong, who emerged as the CCP's leader during the Long March, the epic 1934–1935 retreat of the Communists in the face of attempts by the Nationalists to annihilate them. Mao's new policy would allow autonomy in the minority areas but would not let ethnic minorities create their own states.

The large star on the flag of the People's Republic of China represents the Han nationality; the four smaller stars symbolize important minority groups—specifically, Tibetans, Mongols, Manchus, and Muslims.

China's Minorities Under Communism

From 1937 through 1945, the CCP and the Nationalists were uneasy allies in the war against Japan. But following Japan's surrender, relations between the two parties deteriorated, and civil war broke out in China. By 1949 Mao's Communists had defeated the Nationalists, and in October of that year the People's Republic of China (PRC) was founded. The PRC was (and continues to be) dominated by the CCP, and from the outset its policy toward minorities followed Mao's formulation: ethnic minorities in China would enjoy a degree of autonomy, but they must always remain part of China, secession being absolutely forbidden under any circumstances.

The CCP's notion of autonomy included a measure of political control for the minorities in their own areas. Members of the relevant minority would, for example, hold some of the positions of political power. In addition, there was a cultural component: minorities had the right to use their own languages and to preserve their traditional

A crowd protesting China's invasion of Tibet demonstrates outside the Chinese embassy in New Delhi, India, April 1959. Tibet has presented the most serious challenge to the Chinese government's nationalities policy.

literatures and arts.

In the 1950s, the central government mounted a large-scale "ethnic classification" project. The first step was to invite minority groups to apply for official recognition; more than 400 responded. Government teams then did field investigations and detailed studies to categorize the minorities, using four main criteria. An ethnic minority group was supposed to have 1) a distinct territory; 2) a common language; 3) a common type of economy; and 4) a distinct common culture or psychological makeup. As various Western social scientists have observed, few of the groups that were investigated actually fit all four criteria, but 54 ethnic minorities had nevertheless been recognized by the end of the 1950s. (In 1979, the Jino were added, bringing the total to today's 55.) Members of the would-be ethnic minority groups that did not receive official recognition were sometimes categorized as Han and sometimes classified with other groups considered similar. In addition, some people were

China's 56 Officially Recognized Ethnic Groups

Achang (33,980)
Bai (1.85 million)
Blang (91,900)
Bonan (16,000)
Bouyei (2.97 million)
Dai (1.16 million)
Daur (132,400)
Deang (17,900)
Dong (2.96 million)
Dongxiang (513,800)
Dulong (7,400)
Ewenki (30,500)
Gaoshan (400,000)
Gelao (579,400)
Han
Hani (1.425 million)
Hezhen (4,600)
Hui
Jing (22,500)
Jingpo (132,000)
Jino (20,900)
Kazak (1.25 million)
Kirgiz (160,800)
Korean (1.923 million)
Lahu (453,700)
Lhoba (3,000)
Li (1.25 million)
Lisu (635,000)

Manchu
Maonan (107,200)
Menba (8,900)
Miao
Mongol
Mulam (207,300)
Naxi (308,900)
Nu (28,800)
Oroqen (8,200)
Ozbek (12,400)
Pumi (33,600)
Qiang (306,000)
Russian (15,600)
Salar (104,500)
She (709,600)
Shui (406,900)
Tajik (41,000)
Tatar (4,900)
Tibetan
Tu (241,200)
Tujia (8 million)
Uighur
Wa (396,600)
Xibe (188,800)
Yao
Yi (7.76 million)
Yugur (13,700)
Zhuang

Notes: The nine ethnic groups in boldface are examined in detail in succeeding chapters. Alternate spellings exist for a number of groups. Population figures are from China's 2000 census.
Source: China.org.cn

not categorized as to nationality; in China's 2000 census, the number of people in the unidentified nationality category stood at about three-quarters of a million.

Over the decades, the government established several autonomous administrative regions for minorities. These include the Xinjiang Uighur Autonomous Region, which is populated largely by Muslim minorities of Turkish descent; Tibet (Xizang), home to the Tibetans; the Guangxi Zhuang Autonomous Region, where China's Zhuang minority population is concentrated; Ningxia, home to the Hui, Muslims who have largely assimilated into Han Chinese culture; and Inner Mongolia (Nei Mongol), the northern region where traditionally nomadic Mongols live.

The first, and arguably most serious, test of the CCP's policy of autonomy came in Tibet. The Nationalists, while regarding Tibet as part of China, had in fact exercised virtually no control there. When the CCP came to power, it sent troops to reestablish control in the region. In May 1951, the central government and the local authorities signed an agreement with two main provisions: first, that Tibet would return to China, and second, that its social system would be left intact, with the Tibetans exercising regional autonomy. But during the 1950s, eastern Tibet was wracked by a series of rebellions against Chinese rule. The climax came in March 1959, when a major uprising in Lhasa was suppressed by Chinese troops, with considerable bloodshed. Tibet's leader, the 14th Dalai Lama, fled to India, where he became the focus of a lasting attempt to revive an independent Tibet. One of his arguments against China has been his claim that China is attempting to destroy Tibetan culture.

During the decade-long Cultural Revolution (1966–1976), the CCP policy of autonomy for minorities continued only in theory. In practice, there was a rather drastic reversion toward assimilating minorities into mainstream Han Chinese society. By the 1960s Mao—who was, in a sense, the final arbiter of "mainstream" values—had

This map shows the provinces of China, including the autonomous regions established for some of the country's largest minority groups.

become obsessed with the idea of class struggle, and in unleashing the Cultural Revolution he urged the proletariat (the peasants and working-class laborers) and the young, fervent "Red Guards" militants to root out the supposed enemies of the Chinese Communist revolution: the wealthy, educated elite with their "bourgeois" worldview; "closet capitalists"; reactionaries. In effect, Mao was defining the true "Chinese" identity in terms of class status and devotion to communism, rather than ethnic heritage. Under his policy, differences among the ethnic groups were swept under the carpet in the pursuit of a "pure" Communist state. Religions of all kinds were subject to savage persecution, while the traditional literatures, theaters, and other arts of the ethnic groups were suppressed to make way for revolutionary models.

The Cultural Revolution was discontinued soon after Mao's death in September 1976, and five years later, in June 1981, the CCP formally denounced the Cultural Revolution and virtually everything connected with it. With regard to minority issues China reversed course, reviving and strengthening policies that gave a degree of autonomy to the nationalities. The 1982 Constitution of the People's Republic of China has a good deal to say on the subject of autonomy for the minority areas—in the political, economic, and cultural spheres. It specifies that the government head of all such areas must be a member of the relevant nationality. In addition, it stipulates the right of minorities to use their own spoken and written languages, including in government and the law.

Still, in the late 1980s and early 1990s, the policies of autonomy again came under strain when several attempts at secession were made in the minority areas. The most serious occurred in Tibet, where from 1987 to 1989, major demonstrations, mostly led by monks, erupted in the capital, Lhasa, and elsewhere. The situation, which reached a climax in March 1989, recalled the uprising 30 years earlier. Chinese soldiers crushed the demonstrations, inflicting heavy casualties on the Tibetans. This further damaged relations between the Han majority and the Tibetans, but it also focused international attention on China's treatment of Tibet. Notwithstanding criticism from a host of foreign countries, the Chinese government did not backtrack in its policies.

Despite variations in policy among successive Chinese governments, in one area they have been in striking agreement: all wished to retain China's geographic and national unity. Although the northern part of Mongolia—what is called Outer Mongolia—broke away from China in 1921, it was not until 1945 that the Nationalists finally agreed to acknowledge the independence of the Mongolian People's Republic. And four years later, when they were forced to retreat to Taiwan, the Nationalists rescinded that agreement. As late as the mid-1990s, maps in Taiwan's magnificent National Palace Museum showed China as including northern Mongolia; it was not until 2002 that the Taipei government formally recognized the sovereignty of Mongolia.

By contrast, the People's Republic of China early on recognized the Mongolian People's Republic (and it later accepted that country's 1991 transition to the Republic of Mongolia). However, the Chinese Communist Party proved just as steadfast as the Nationalists in insisting on the indivisibility of all of the country's remaining territory. Whatever had been part of the Qing dynasty's realm at the end of the 19th century—including Tibet, Xinjiang, and Inner Mongolia—was seen as integral to China. And through its stated policy as well as concrete actions, the CCP has continued to make clear that it will not tolerate attempts at secession.

In general, the Chinese state has, over the course of its history, consolidated its hold over ethnic minorities—and the integration of minorities within China accelerated during the second half of the 20th century. Still, some frictions will undoubtedly persist—and may well erupt periodically into open conflict—as the government's goal of national unity and ethnic integration runs up against the sense of identity and national aspirations of certain minority peoples within China's borders.

Chinese political leaders, including former president Jiang Zemin (left) and current president Hu Jintao (right), listen as the chairman of the Chinese People's Political Consultative Conference, Jia Qinglin, gives a speech. Most of the country's top leaders come from the Han ethnic group.

2

The Ruling Han

Chinese civilization—which is closely associated with the group that is today referred to as the Han people—first began to develop along the Yellow River, where agricultural settlements existed from Neolithic times. Precisely where the Han originally came from is unknown, but evidence strongly suggests that they lived in areas that are today within China's borders for a long time. Anthropologists believe that the Han Chinese resulted from the fusion of more than one cultural group. The group that supplied the language form now called Chinese branched off from an earlier group that was also ancestral—linguistically speaking—to the Tibeto-Burman peoples.

Origins of the Han

Today China is overwhelmingly composed of Han Chinese, with all the other ethnic groups constituting only about 8.4 percent of the population. It is the elements of Han civilization, named after the Han dynasty (206 B.C–A.D. 221), that have become synonymous with Chinese civilization. Although ethnic groups such as the Mongols and the Manchus conquered the Han majority (and ruled for about 90 years and more than 250 years, respectively), they inevitably defaulted to the Han culture in their attempts to consolidate their power and dominance over the majority.

While the name of the Han ethnic group is derived from the dynasty that was founded in the late third century B.C., the civilization of the Han Chinese actually dates back much further. Scholars cannot establish exactly when Han civilization began, but the Han Chinese have long traced their origins to the legendary ruler Huang Di ("the Yellow Emperor"); even today, the Han Chinese often refer to themselves as sons of the Yellow Emperor. The first Chinese surnames supposedly came from the names that Huang Di gave his 25 sons. According to legend, Huang Di personally devised, or encouraged his subjects to create, a host of fundamental advances that formed the foundation of a flourishing civilization, including the wheel, writing, the calendar, fabric clothing, and even the magnetic compass. He and his four legendary heirs—including the brothers Yao and Shun, who were said to have ruled during a golden age of early Chinese civilization—are traditionally credited with establishing a central civilization surrounded by barbarian tribesmen. This would become a recurring theme in Chinese history.

Modern archaeology supports a more gradual view of Chinese cultural advancement than that offered by the legends surrounding the Yellow Emperor and his successors. For about four centuries beginning around 2000 B.C., a dynasty known as the Xia ruled a relatively small area near the southern bend of the Yellow River. The Xia, whose use of bronze enabled them to conquer neighbors armed only with stone and wood weapons, developed a complex, specialized society with elaborate rituals that legitimized the power of the ruling class. Around 1600 B.C., another bronze-making culture, the Shang, displaced the Xia and extended their power over a larger swath of territory. Like their predecessors, the Shang emphasized ritual (ancestor worship became particularly important). Shang rule appears to have been rather harsh, but significant cultural advances, such as the extensive use of writing, were also made. Around 1027 B.C., the Shang dynasty was overthrown and the Zhou dynasty established. Although the Zhou dynasty would in theory last into the latter part of the third century B.C., during most of that time it exerted little or no actual control over its realm. From 770 B.C. onward, China was wracked by continual warfare and social chaos as the lords of various feudal states fought one another for supremacy.

Eventually the state of Qin emerged victorious, and China was unified in 221 B.C. But the brutally repressive Qin dynasty lasted a scant 15 years before being overthrown.

In its wake, the Han dynasty ushered in an extended period of stability. It was during this time that the official Han identity emerged as a recognized group, distinct from the nomads in the north and the mountain people in the south. To assert control over all of China, the Han rulers greatly needed doctrines that would support both their own legitimacy and the political unity of the Chinese-language community. The project of history writing filled this need.

The earlier history of the Chinese peoples was gathered and sifted, and past events, even ancient legends, were carefully reinterpreted to provide the needed moral underpinnings of a unified Han state and identity. Confucian values—including the importance of education, reciprocity in social relations, and obedience to legitimate authority—were stressed. Under the doctrine of the "Mandate of Heaven," the ruling dynasty was seen to exercise a divine right to govern as long as it did so properly. The Han envisioned a concentric world at the

From the days of the Han dynasty (206 B.C.–A.D. 220) until the 20th century, the teachings of Confucius (551–479 B.C.) formed the basis for Chinese government and society.

center of which was the emperor. The sovereign leader of the one legitimate state under Heaven— Zhongguo, or the Middle Kingdom— the emperor ruled the world's civilized people; all the lands surrounding this realm were populated by "barbarians." As the Son of Heaven, the emperor performed the rites needed to keep Earth in harmony with Heaven. This relationship was believed to mirror the Confucian duties that a good son should perform for his father and other ancestors in order to keep the present in harmony with the past.

The concept of the Mandate of Heaven incorporated the idea that political unity should be the norm in China. And it seemed natural, under this model, for the Han to be at the center of the unified China. Using the name of the dynasty to also designate the ethnic group was a deliberate attempt to identify the Han as the civilized people of the Middle Kingdom, separate from the "barbarians." With that label, the Han people assumed the status of majority Chinese identity, a designation that survives to the present day.

Constructing the Han Identity

The adoption of a single language and especially a standard system of writing, which was ordered by the first Qin emperor, proved perhaps the most important factor in the creation and maintenance of a unified Han Chinese cultural identity. Although the Chinese written script was cumbersome, it made possible communication among all educated people in the Middle Kingdom, regardless of any differences in spoken language. (Even today, the written script enables all Chinese to communicate with one another, even if their spoken languages or dialects are mutually unintelligible.)

The Han objective was not unlike that of the Communist leaders of contemporary China: to integrate outside groups into their civilization. Alliances were formed by marriage; elite groups from among the barbarian tribesmen were provided education in *hanzi*, the Chinese writing system. The adoption of recognized Han rites and customs was encouraged in the context of broadening and deepening the dominance of Han as the culture of China. Barbarian individuals and groups that accepted the language and ideology of the Han were from then on treated as *Hanren*, Han people. The test of who was a Han was not necessarily racial, but based on social construct and language. And, in a sense, it has remained this way up until the present day, with only minor exceptions.

But the Han identity, while solid, was challenged throughout the years. Ironically, the Han faced the same challenge as today's Chinese leaders: the diversity of China's cultures cannot be ignored or buried simply by unifying the language and social structure. The Han Chinese have long struggled to impose order and system upon the complex and changing mosaic of "barbarian peoples" around them. Disintegration of the Han dynasty's political system began with the revolt of the Yellow Turbans in the northeast in A.D. 184. The collapse of the dynasty in 220 thrust China into almost 400 years of political division.

Solidifying the Han Identity

The revival of a dominant Han political ideology and cultural tradition did not resurface until 1368, under the Ming dynasty. The Ming rulers carried on with the Han dynastic tradition of assimilating

The Temple of Heaven in Beijing was built during the Ming dynasty (1368–1644) as a place for the emperor to worship his ancestors and pray for a good harvest. This was an important part of the Han social system, in which the emperor needed to keep Earth and Heaven in harmony.

"barbarians" into the Han Chinese identity. In particular, they paid special attention to incorporating the Muslim population into mainstream society. By the Ming era, there were many Central Asian Muslims in China who spoke local Chinese dialects rather than Arabic, Turkic, or other non-Chinese languages. The Ming encouraged the Islamic population to adopt at least the outer trappings of Han culture, and their success in promoting Chinese language and education among Muslims is today reflected in the Hui minority group. During Ming rule, most Hui took Chinese surnames. In the eras to follow, many Hui looked back on the Ming period as a golden age of prosperity and community expansion.

Toward the end of the Ming dynasty, the rulers' corruption and insularity began to erode the unified Han identity that emperors over the centuries had worked hard to build. The Ming emperors faced the same challenges as their predecessors in trying to appease, co-opt, or overpower the non-Han peoples who lived on the fringes of China. During the 1520s, the Ming saw bloody peasant revolts and continuing warfare with the Mongols and other northern nomadic groups. In the end, continual infighting within the ruling elites of the Ming dynasty created an opening for the northeastern Manchus to topple imperial Ming rule.

The population of China increased considerably during the Manchu Qing dynasty, but it also fragmented along social and ethnic lines as the Manchus tried to assert the supremacy of their culture in China. To control the diverse mosaic of ethnicities in China, the Manchu rulers followed a divide-and-rule policy, playing the Muslim Hui off against the Han, for example, and creating tensions among ethnic groups so as to prevent any unified front that could challenge their dominance. Yet ironically, the Manchus also adopted the Han court system as well as its education and commerce systems, which some scholars say made them "more Han than the Han." Even so, throughout the Manchu Qing dynasty, the Han majority organized dozens of rebellions to take back what they saw as their rightful power to rule over China. "Oppose the Qing, Revive the Ming" became the predominant slogan that helped the Han preserve their identity under what they saw as "alien rule."

Today's Han

Is it really possible to speak of an ethnic Han identity that includes all but 8.4 percent of modern China's 1.35 billion people— particularly in light of the intermarriage, political alliances, and migrations of ethnic groups across the country that occurred in China over the centuries? In so many ways (as numerous scholars have pointed out), the ethnic Han identity of today's China is socially constructed—as it was in the days of the Han dynasty and then in the Ming dynasty—as an assertion of political power over the rest of the population, rather than as a cultural identity that unifies. On the surface it seems that linguistically, the unifying characteristic of the Han people is Mandarin Chinese. But even under that umbrella, the predominantly Chinese-speaking Hui ethnic Muslims must be separated out. And then there are the dialects of the Mandarin Chinese language that are spoken in specific regions of the country (and that are not necessarily intelligible elsewhere in China). In the south, for example, the Cantonese have developed their own colloquial language; the Shanghainese, living in the commercial center of China, also have their own dialect.

If language is no longer at the center of Han identity, as it was 2,000 years ago during the Han dynasty, on what basis do a billion Chinese believe themselves members of the same ethnic group? It seems, as many scholars have asserted, that the Han identity has evolved into one based on nationalism.

Writing shortly after the birth of the Chinese republic in the early 1910s, Sun Yat-sen, the revolutionary who ended China's dynastic rule and instituted a modern government, asserted that the state and the nation (the people) meant the same thing in China, where a single state (the political entity) developed from a single race. "Although there are a little over ten million non-Han in China, including Mongols, Manchus, Tibetans, and Tatars," Sun maintained, "their number is small compared with the purely Han population. . . . China is one nationality." As for those who did not belong to the Han race, Sun believed that they should be kept within the state but urged to assimilate. While acknowledging the presence of distinct minority groups, Sun and other Chinese leaders to follow would insist that the Han identity dominate what it means to be Chinese.

Mao's policy on assimilation of ethnic minorities to conform to the Han identity was subtle and hidden behind the veil of class struggle. Beginning in the late 1960s, Mao sent urban youth to the countryside to be "reeducated" by poor and lower-middle-class peasants. Before the policy of "rustification" was abandoned the following decade, an estimated 15 million youth had been dispatched to the countryside. It is unclear how many were sent to minority areas, though some scholars believe that part of the policy's goal was to assimilate ethnic minorities by swamping them with Han colonists.

When classifying an ethnic group, the immediate instinct seems to be to single out its differences; the more dramatic these differences, the clearer the ethnic boundaries can be drawn. With the Han people, ethnic lines seem to blur amid a culture shared by more than a billion people. Chinese government policy toward ethnicity has always been to excise all that is not Han. What is left, logically, must be what makes the Han people Han—and perhaps in the end this is as close as one can get to defining Han identity.

A Han family poses for a photo in front of a model of China's *Shenzhou V* spacecraft at a Hong Kong science museum.

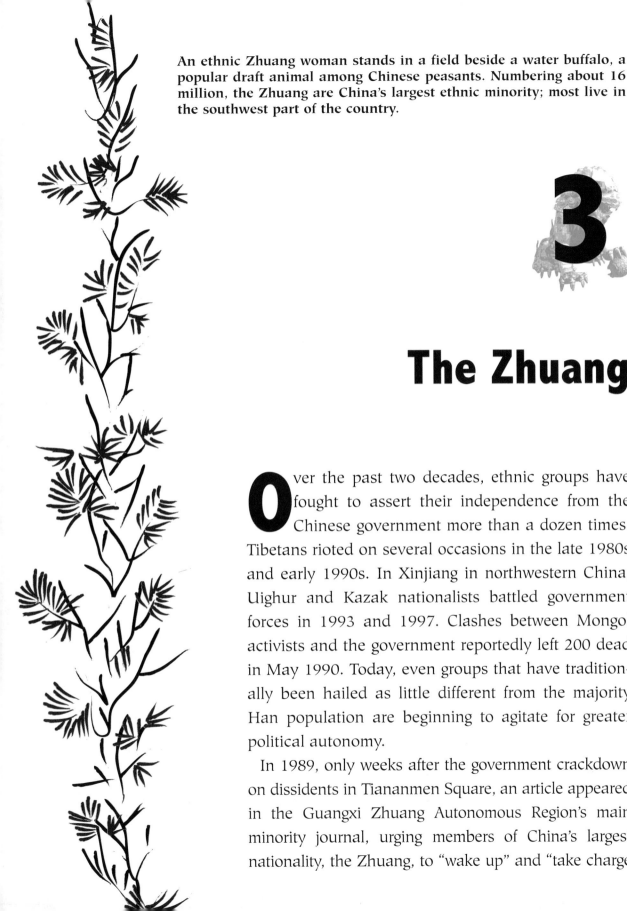

An ethnic Zhuang woman stands in a field beside a water buffalo, a popular draft animal among Chinese peasants. Numbering about 16 million, the Zhuang are China's largest ethnic minority; most live in the southwest part of the country.

3

The Zhuang

Over the past two decades, ethnic groups have fought to assert their independence from the Chinese government more than a dozen times. Tibetans rioted on several occasions in the late 1980s and early 1990s. In Xinjiang in northwestern China, Uighur and Kazak nationalists battled government forces in 1993 and 1997. Clashes between Mongol activists and the government reportedly left 200 dead in May 1990. Today, even groups that have traditionally been hailed as little different from the majority Han population are beginning to agitate for greater political autonomy.

In 1989, only weeks after the government crackdown on dissidents in Tiananmen Square, an article appeared in the Guangxi Zhuang Autonomous Region's main minority journal, urging members of China's largest nationality, the Zhuang, to "wake up" and "take charge of the leadership in Guangxi." In January 1991, some 270 Guangxi Zhuang intellectuals and government officials announced the formation of the first non-governmental Zhuang Studies Association. Two years later, more than 500 Zhuang in neighboring Yunnan Province petitioned the government for recognition of an independent Yunnan Zhuang Studies Association. In the southwestern provinces bordering Vietnam, publications began to print demands for legal guarantees for Zhuang autonomy, bilingual education for Zhuang children, and greater Zhuang control of government positions. China's largest ethnic minority has now found a voice among the dozens of ethnic groups vying for more political and economic autonomy from the central government.

Who Are the Zhuang?

Numbering some 16 million, the Zhuang are China's largest ethnic minority; only five other minority groups have a population exceeding 8 million, and none of them tops 11 million. The Zhuang people live mostly in southwest China, in the Guangxi Zhuang Autonomous Region and Yunnan Province. More than 1,000 kilometers (620 miles) of Zhuang territory borders Vietnam, making the local population's loyalty to the Chinese state of particular strategic concern to Beijing.

Even so, the Zhuang have long been casually dismissed by scholars in the West as assimilated and fully integrated into the Han majority. Today, however, Zhuang peasants, intellectuals, workers, and cadres proudly assert their membership in an ancient and culturally rich minority group. After nearly two millennia of alternating preferential and discriminatory policies, the Zhuang have been pushed into geographically hostile regions, where they live in depressed economic conditions relative to their Han counterparts. Education levels among the Zhuang are significantly below the nationwide average, and they remain locked in agricultural subsistence economies while their Han neighbors rush to seize the advantages of a rapidly developing market economy. Zhuang intellectuals are adamant in their demand that the Zhuang written script be promoted throughout Zhuang territory, as part of an effort to "regain" control of their history, which they claim has been expropriated by Han historiography (history writing).

So who are these mysterious Zhuang? Do they, in fact, constitute a "unique nationality"? Or are they simply, as one Western scholar has suggested, a purely artificial and recent construct?

A group of boys sits on a stoop in Guilin, a city in the northeastern part of the Guangxi Zhuang Autonomous Region. The government's attempts to construct a unified Zhuang identity have been largely frustrated by the tendency of Zhuang people to define themselves according to membership in one of three subgroups: the Nong, Sha, or Tu. Each has its own distinctive clothing and customs.

The Invisible Ethnic Minority

The cause of the Zhuang enigma is not difficult to ascertain. None of the regimes preceding the Communists actually recognized the Zhuang as an ethnic nationality. Not until the early 1950s did the Zhuang identity begin to emerge, and that identity was solidified with the formation of the Guangxi Zhuang Autonomous Region.

The Zhuang are concentrated almost exclusively in western Guangxi and eastern Yunnan, with small patches of communities in eastern Guangxi and western Guangdong. Before the early 1950s, many of those now considered Zhuang did not perceive of themselves as such. The boundaries of what constitutes Zhuang ethnicity (as with any ethnic group in China) have been created and continually re-created over the centuries. But where did the Zhuang come from originally?

Historians disagree on the answer to that question. Some argue that the Zhuang came from the north or west; others suggest that they may have originated in west-central China. Still others say they were the original inhabitants of Guangxi, where they are concentrated now. In any event, the first references to the Zhuang appeared during the Han dynasty (206 B.C.–A.D. 220). The name then disappeared for hundreds of years and resurfaced again around 1000; throughout history, scholars writing about minority people in Guangxi seldom mentioned the Zhuang.

Isolation and Integration

Historically, the peoples living in western Guangxi were largely isolated by the region's harsh, mountainous terrain, and Zhuang economic, cultural, and administrative integration with the rest of China remained minimal. Within the Zhuang community, there were three main branches of identity—the Nong, the Sha, and the Tu—and over the years subdivisions within each of the three branches emerged.

Today these affiliations remain more pronounced in Yunnan

Province than in Guangxi. Few of the Zhuang in Yunnan actually refer to themselves as "Zhuang"; rather, they are more likely to see themselves as members of the Nong, Sha, or Tu. And just as they would deny an overarching Zhuang identity, many would also reject their Chinese nationality.

Folk legend in Yunnan explains that the Nong, Sha, and Tu descended from three brothers. The Nong brother was the eldest and lived as a farmer along the river. The middle brother, ancestor of the Sha, was also a farmer but settled along the edge of a lake. The Tu brother, the legend holds, was just an infant when the brothers' parents died and their household had to separate. This legend reflects the relative socioeconomic position each branch holds in Yunnan society. The Nong, numerically dominant, also view themselves as socially superior to the other two branches.

The Chinese government has discouraged open discussion of, or emphasis on, the differences among the branches, preferring to lump the three groups under a unifying Zhuang identity. But it is not difficult to identify members of the respective branches simply by differences in the way they dress. The Nong, for example, typically wear dark-colored pants and a blue smock with buttons running down the right side from the shoulder. The upper center of the smock is often embroidered in the elaborate knotted-brocade design on which the Nong pride themselves. The women wear a floral towel twisted on their heads. Although few women in the cities or county capitals wear traditional minority dress, in many villages the characteristic blue is the only color of apparel to be found. The proportion of women wearing minority clothing increases the further removed a village is from the nearest city.

The Sha do not wear the blue smocks and pants of the Nong, nor do they use towels as head covering. They often wear more elaborate silver hairpieces that drape down their backs in square-paneled designs.

Zhuang women wearing traditional garb hold onto their headgear on a windy day in Beijing's Tiananmen Square.

Tu women frequently wear long black dresses, mostly while they are working in the rice fields or fishing. The Tu take great pride in the unique embroidery of their minority costumes, which are very different from those of the Nong. Whereas the Nong patterns are flowing designs, often with representations of animals and birds, the Tu patterns are geometric, in vibrant triangles and squares of fuchsia, green, electric blue, and purple. The Tu headdress is also distinctive. The typical Tu woman wears a dark head wrapping that entirely covers the head and is held in place with a vibrant embroidered band.

The distinct modes of dress among the Nong, Sha, and Tu are not the only clue that the conception of a unified Zhuang nationality is lacking. Another telling indicator is the plethora of names by which different communities refer to themselves. There are at least 20 such names used by Zhuang in different areas.

Unlike the Tibetans or Muslims in northwestern China, the Zhuang do not have a unified religion, which has further inhibited their integration as a single nationality. The Zhuang are animists; they worship a variety of spirits (along with ancestors), but no single spirit is worshiped by all, nor is there a hierarchical religious leadership that ties together the different villages.

The Zhuang in China Today

Long neglected, the Zhuang came into the spotlight after the founding of the People's Republic of China in 1949. Political considerations factored heavily into which groups the new regime would label Zhuang, and some coercion was used to convince local ethnic leaders to accept the classification. Under the new government, the previously unrecognized Zhuang nationality was officially granted numerous rights, including the right to govern its own internal affairs, to have proportional representation in local and national political organizations, and to develop its language and culture. In 1958, the Chinese government expanded the territory under Zhuang control and announced the establishment of the Guangxi Zhuang Autonomous Region, one of only five provincial-level autonomous units in the country. The government's incentives and coercive measures appear to have paid off. In 1953, when asked to declare their nationality, only 6.61 million people registered as Zhuang; by 1990, the number of registered Zhuang stood at 15 million.

The Zhuang often say that they lack a sense of ethnic identity because they have had no heroes. Seeking to build Zhuang cohesion and pride—as well as to emphasize the supposed historical cooperation between the Zhuang and their "Han big brothers"— the Chinese government began to develop a gallery of Zhuang heroes after 1952. Various figures, both historical and legendary, were hailed as symbols of the "great contribution" the "Zhuang nationality" had made to the motherland.

Significantly, none of the historical figures had actually ever addressed the Zhuang as a people, or even emphasized their nationality. Yet the Communist Party wove details from these individuals' lives into a narrative that supported the objectives of the Party's minority policies. Perhaps the best example of this is the Party's treatment of Wei Baqun.

Born in 1894, Wei led a series of peasant uprisings in 1923 in western Guangxi's Zhuang-dominated Donglan County. Seizing on the opportunities presented by the peasant movement in Donglan, the Chinese Communist Party's central leadership sent representatives to the area in the late 1920s to establish a revolutionary base. The peasant movement, which expanded throughout much of western Guangxi, became known as the Baise Uprising. After 1949, the Party began a massive propaganda campaign to honor the achievements of Wei Baqun. Mao Zedong himself hailed Wei as the "son of the Zhuang people" and "great leader of the peasantry."

In addition to its efforts to create Zhuang national heroes, the Chinese government tried (delicately) to promote Zhuang ethnic traditions and festivals—as long as they did not perpetuate deep cultural differences and thereby threaten the Chinese Communist Party's conception of "national unity." Sanyuesan Festival (the March Third Festival), for example, was merely a limited village festival before the Chinese Communist Party transformed it into a dominant celebration of Zhuang culture. Held on the third day of the third lunar month, the festival lasts one or two days and is most notable for the singing of Zhuang mountain songs. Traditionally the mountain songs were spontaneous: one singer would improvise words, often in the form of a riddle or romantic proposition, and the responding singer, without missing a rhythmic beat, would have to respond to the first singer before adding his or her own lyrics.

Consolidating the Zhuang Identity

Guangxi's rugged geography has historically stood in the way of a developed transportation and communications infrastructure. Until the middle of the 20th century, the Zhuang economy revolved around small-scale, self-sufficient farming. In 1949, less than 1 percent of the Zhuang population was engaged in non-agricultural labor. And because of the practically nonexistent infrastructure, farmers rarely traded with villages outside walking distance. After years of devastation by civil war and the war against the Japanese, what little infrastructure Guangxi had was in shambles when the Chinese Communists took over. Their priority of repairing roads, railroads, and waterways ultimately gave the Zhuang a link to the rest of China.

After more than 50 years of Chinese Communist Party rule, the political identity of the people living in western Guangxi and eastern

Historically, most residents of the Guangxi Zhuang Autonomous Region, like this peasant, have been farmers.

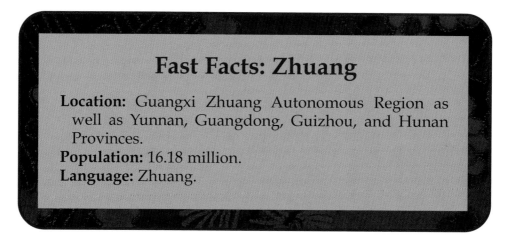

Fast Facts: Zhuang

Location: Guangxi Zhuang Autonomous Region as well as Yunnan, Guangdong, Guizhou, and Hunan Provinces.
Population: 16.18 million.
Language: Zhuang.

Yunnan has been radically transformed. It is not simply that the previously remote, predominantly self-sufficient farming communities have now begun to participate in China's budding, integrated market economy. A half-century ago many of western Guangxi's villages, surrounded by high stony mountains, were cut off not only from the rest of China but also from the other villages in the region. Thus many villagers had little sense of belonging to a larger group; few had ever even heard the term *Zhuang.* Today more than 16 million boast of their membership in China's largest minority nationality.

Much of this transformation can be attributed to the Chinese Communist Party's desire to consolidate its hold over southwestern China. The central government made the political calculation that promoting a Zhuang nationality, and then granting that nationality one of the country's only five provincial-level autonomous units, was the best—perhaps the only—means of integrating the diverse southern peoples into a unified Chinese state system. By awarding the Zhuang autonomy, the Party believed, it could both increase their commitment to the Chinese Communist Party and the People's Republic of China and aid in developing their political, cultural, and economic position within that unified state. The government essentially gave the Zhuang its nationality and a voice, all in the name of integrating the Chinese nation.

Only two ethnic groups, the Tibetans and the small Muslim minority in western Xinjiang, have histories of independent statehood. The social reconstruction of the Zhuang as a nationality elevated the status of a group that did not previously have an identity; at the same time, however, it relegated the group to a status lower than that of the dominant Han people. And, despite recent Zhuang demands for greater autonomy, there is relatively little chance that the Zhuang will mobilize to secede, as the Tibetans and Uighurs have attempted to do repeatedly. Divisions among the Nong, Sha, and Tu branches, along with the scattered geography of the Zhuang population—not to mention the central government's enormous coercive power—would give pause to anyone contemplating a Zhuang separatist movement. In any case, it seems that the Zhuang do not have the same aspirations as the Uighurs and Tibetans. For now at least, simple recognition, after remaining in the shadows for so long, seems to be a big enough step.

This Qing dynasty painting shows a nobleman and his wife. Established in 1644 by the Manchus, the Qing dynasty ruled China until the early 20th century but was always resented by the majority Han people.

The Manchus

The Manchus figure prominently in almost any discussion of modern Chinese history. A non-Han people originally from what is now China's northeastern frontier, they established China's last imperial dynasty, the Qing (1644–1911). One writer has described Manchu rule as a shaping force that "generated a strong sense of nationalistic racial consciousness among Chinese." Thus the Manchus played a major (if unintentional) role in creating the unified, modern China that exists today.

Throughout their three centuries as rulers of China, the Manchus were preoccupied with three basic goals: securing legitimacy and support from the majority Han Chinese, preserving their own ethnic identity, and achieving military conquest. Today, the Manchu identity has largely faded. Northeast China—previously known as Manchuria, after the dominant group there—is now home mainly to Han Chinese, along with a mix of Koreans, Mongols, and Manchus.

The relationship between the Han Chinese and the Manchus—or, as they were called until the 17th century, the Jurchen (Nuzhen in the pinyin system of transliterating Chinese characters)—has always been one of patronage, tension, and loose alliances. Over the course of many centuries, tribal leaders pledged their allegiance to emperors of the various Han Chinese dynasties. In return, they were mostly left alone to pursue their horseback-riding, nomadic lifestyle. But in the 12th century, the Jurchen founded the Jin, or Kin ("Gold"), dynasty in Manchuria, and it challenged the supremacy of China's Southern Song dynasty.

In the 13th century, however, the Mongols—fearsome horsemen from the central Asian steppes—conquered China and established the Yuan dynasty. Throughout the Yuan dynasty, which lasted from 1279 to 1368, the people of Manchuria were under Mongol control. But after the downfall of the Yuan dynasty, the Jurchen regained much of their independence.

Although the Jurchen represented a separate, semi-nomadic cultural tradition for most of their history, during the 14th and 15th centuries, they increasingly adopted Chinese culture, eating habits, and living habits. In the 16th century, Chinese crossing over from the southeast in Liaotung taught the Jurchen how to build forts and how to farm. The importation of technology and agriculture converted the Jurchen from a largely nomadic culture to a sedentary one. The stage was set for the emergence of the Jurchen as a major cultural force in Asia. All that would be required was a strong leader.

That leader was Nurhachi (1559–1626), who unified the Jurchen people and mounted a series of military campaigns against the Chinese Ming dynasty. After Nurhachi's death, his son Abahai (known also as Huang Taiji) continued the invasion of China and renamed his people the Manchus. Abahai died in 1643, just a year before the Manchu conquest of China was completed.

The Manchu Qing ("Pure") dynasty would endure for more than 250 years. But throughout all that time, it was bitterly resented as a foreign, occupying dynasty.

China Under Manchu Rule

Although the Manchus were not Han and were strongly resisted, especially in the south, they had absorbed a great deal of Chinese culture before conquering China Proper (basically the territory within the Great Wall). And they realized that to rule the empire, they would have to do things the Chinese way. For that reason the Manchus retained many institutions of Ming and earlier Chinese derivation. They continued the Confucian court practices and temple rituals, over which the Chinese emperors had traditionally presided. The Manchus also continued the Confucian civil service system. Although Han Chinese were barred from the highest offices, they constituted the majority of officeholders outside the capital (except in military positions). The Manchus also enforced as the state creed Neo-Confucian philosophy, which emphasized the obedience of subject to ruler; this was an attempt to bolster the legitimacy of their control over the majority Han. But the Manchu emperors also supported Chinese literary and historical projects of enormous scope. In fact, the survival of much of China's ancient literature is attributable to these projects.

The Qing rulers put into effect measures aimed at preventing the absorption of the Manchus into the dominant Han Chinese population. Han Chinese were prohibited from migrating into the Manchu homeland, and Manchus were forbidden to engage in trade or manual labor. Intermarriage between the two groups was strictly forbidden. In many government positions, a system of dual appointments was used—the Chinese appointee was required to do the substantive work, and the Manchu to ensure Han loyalty to Qing rule.

Manchus from the Qing court pose with Europeans, circa 1902. Although they adopted Confucian ways to secure legitimacy among the Han Chinese they ruled, the Manchus also tried to preserve their ethnic identity. Intermarriage with the Han was strictly forbidden.

The Qing regime was determined to protect itself not only from internal rebellion but also from foreign invasion. After China Proper had been subdued, the Manchus conquered Outer Mongolia (now the Republic of Mongolia) in the late 17th century. In the 18th century, they gained control of Central Asia as far as the Pamir Mountains and established a protectorate over the area the Chinese call Xizang (commonly known in the West as Tibet). The Qing thus became the first dynasty to eliminate successfully all danger to China Proper from across its land borders. Under Manchu rule, the empire grew to include a larger area than before or since; Taiwan, the last outpost of anti-Manchu resistance, was also incorporated into China for the first time. In addition, Qing emperors received tribute from the various border states.

The chief threat to China's territorial integrity did not come overland, as it had so often in the past, but by sea. Western traders, missionaries, and soldiers of fortune began to arrive in large numbers in the southern coastal area even before the Qing, in the 16th century. The empire's inability to evaluate correctly the nature of the new challenge or to respond flexibly to it resulted in the demise of the Qing and the collapse of the entire millennia-old framework of dynastic rule.

Myths of Manchu Origins

The ethnic roots of the Manchus are not entirely clear. Much is hidden by a shroud of secrecy created by the Qing court in the mid-18th century, when the court was anxious to project a unified imperial image onto a fragmented and humble past and was in a position to edit some of the historical materials. One approach to the question of Manchu origins is to consider briefly the circumstances surrounding the history of the Manchus as a minority group in China today.

A few years after the founding of the People's Republic of China in 1949, the Manchus were officially recognized as a "minority nationality," in theory distinguished from the majority Han nationality on the basis of four defining characteristics: territory, language, economy, and culture or psychological nature. Since most Manchus left their native land for China in the 1600s, and since all but a tiny fraction had lost the ability to speak the Manchu language (and in many other ways had become highly acculturated), demonstrating one's "Manchu-ness" was not always easy. Nonetheless, in 1953 some 2.4 million people nationwide were registered as Manchus, the majority in Beijing and in northeastern China. Twenty-five years later, a 1978 survey revealed that this number had grown by 10 percent, to 2.65 million. At the time of the first "modern" census in 1982, however, the Manchu population had risen to 4.3 million; in 1987, the number had increased again to 7 million, almost three times what it had been just nine years before. Astonishingly, in

1993, the figure rose further, to a total of 9.82 million—more than four times the number of Manchus reported 40 years before. The 2000 Chinese census counted 10.68 million Manchus, making them the second most numerous minority population.

The skyrocketing rate of Manchu population growth obviously cannot be explained by normal rates of reproduction. Owing partly to liberal state policies toward official non-Han minorities, many people who formerly preferred to hide their Manchu past have apparently decided to declare it openly. In addition, some claiming Manchu ethnic status today evidently did not think of themselves as Manchus before; nor can they trace their descent from a Manchu clan. Some studies indicate that a great number of people who in recent years have decided to identify themselves as Manchus are Han Chinese whose ancestors were registered somewhere within the banner system, which the Qing rulers used to organize and control military brigades. Many of these new registrants might have been descendants of servants and agricultural workers living in Manchu households. But their historical association with the Eight Banners qualifies them to choose ethnic status as Manchus under China's minority nationality laws.

These Manchu women are dressed in traditional clothing. Today China has more than 10 million Manchus, making them the country's second-largest ethnic minority group.

Fast Facts: Manchus

Location: mainly Liaoning Province, as well as Jilin, Heilongjiang, Hebei, Gansu, Shandong, Inner Mongolia, Xinjiang, and Ningxia.
Population: 10.68 million.
Language: ancient Manchu script and language, belonging to the Manchu-Tungusic group of the Altaic language family (but that language is largely disappearing).

The story that the Manchus liked to tell about their origins centered on the legend of three heavenly maidens, Enggulen, Jenggulen, and Fekulen. According to the legend, the three sisters descended one day from Heaven to bathe in a lake at the foot of Mount Bukuri (later said to be in the Changbai Mountains, near the modern Chinese border with Korea). When they emerged from the water, the youngest of them, Fekulen, found a magical red fruit on top of her clothing. The fruit had been placed there by a magpie, a spirit-messenger from the Lord of Heaven. Having nowhere to put the fruit while she dressed, and finding it very attractive, she placed it for a moment in her mouth. As soon as she had done this, however, it passed down her throat and her body suddenly became "heavy"—she had conceived a child. Her sisters returned to Heaven, while she assumed a human form and later gave birth to a male child whom she named Bukuri Yongson, the progenitor of the Manchu ruling house. The story continues by explaining how Bukuri Yongson became the leader of the Jurchen.

Who Are the Real Manchus?

The name "Manchu" and the creation of a unified state came about at virtually the same time—in the 1630s, when the Manchus were close to conquering all of China. Previously, the only word for the people now known as the Manchus was *Jurchen*. Living largely in the northeast parts of China and further into Russia, the Jurchen were forest dwellers. The traditional Jurchen way of life was a blend of the pastoral and sedentary, combining hunting and fishing with nomadism and agriculture, supplemented by the tributary trade to which they were entitled as subjects of the ruling Chinese dynasty. Until Nurhachi came into power in the 1600s, the Jurchen were a scattered tribe of people, the various clans within the tribe living on their own, with little cooperation or unified tribal identity.

Like the Mongol conqueror Genghis Khan (also spelled Chinggis Khan), Nurhachi relied on the mechanism of "companionhood" to unite his people. Through this idea, he developed what is perhaps the most famous of Manchu institutions: the Eight Banners. The banner system was above all a way for Nurhachi to field a potent military force, but the banners also organized the Manchu people's political and economic life. A banner consisted of many basic units called *niulu,* each of which incorporated about 300 men. In wartime the members of a *niulu* went into battle together; in peacetime they hunted or farmed together.

By the mid-1600s, Nurhachi's army had expanded so greatly that it began to incorporate new banners of Mongols and Han Chinese soldiers. The original banners were known as the Manchu Eight Banners, a designation meant to distinguish the Manchus clearly from all others. The fully formed banner system consisted of about two dozen banners.

The formation of the banner system was an innovation of major importance. A banner constituted the social, economic, and political network of its men, as well as their families. At the beginning of the Qing dynasty, the Manchus were acutely aware that they were seen as foreign invaders and alien rulers. To generate support and consent among the majority Han Chinese, the Manchus created banners for them, as well as for Mongols, Koreans, and other ethnic minorities. Thus it might be said that the Qing state recognized diversity and provided a "home" for the ethnic groups within its borders—even though the banners of other ethnic groups clearly enjoyed a lesser status than the original Manchu Eight Banners.

Still, the banner system was the quintessential way in which the Manchus asserted and protected their identity, in particular by imparting a set of practices in daily life that effectively divided the original Manchu banner people from Han Chinese. The banner

A Manchu bride and groom leave the hall during their wedding in Harbin, Heilongjiang Province.

system separated people physically in the Manchu cities. It marked the Manchus economically, granting them a status in Qing society that was both separate and privileged, especially where the Manchu banners were concerned. Occupationally as well, the banner system specified what its constituents might do in life, forbidding them any profession other than soldier, clerk, or official. In exchange, it extended them various considerations that worked very much to their advantage in the intense competition to enter government service. The banners also conferred a separate legal status; bannermen enjoyed general immunity from normal civil prosecution and automatically qualified for lenient treatment and lightening of penalties. The banners were an explicitly ethnic institution; together with various defining Manchu cultural practices, it was the Eight Banners that enabled the survival of the Manchus as a distinct, coherent group bound by shared lifestyles, shared institutions, and a belief in a shared past.

Yet the Manchus recognized that ethnicity was an unstable basis for politics and power. In public, among the Han Chinese, they preferred to wear a Confucian face, professing their impartiality toward the distinction between Manchu and Han. However, as they adopted the Chinese court system and Chinese customs as a way of gaining mass support, the Manchu identity itself was jeopardized. In ruling China, the Manchus—whether unknowingly or deliberately—tried to find a balance between preserving their identity and unifying diverse ethnicities. In some ways, the whole idea of a multiethnic state in China began with the Manchus.

The governments that came after the fall of the Manchu Qing dynasty in 1911 all purported to create a unified but multiethnic Chinese state. In 1949, when the Chinese Communist Party took power and founded the People's Republic of China, CCP officials described the country as a state in which many nationalities were united. In expanding the number of ethnic groups it recognized to

56 and in promising equality to all of them, the Chinese government certainly departed from the Manchu way, but the Manchu hand could still clearly be felt in the recognition of ethnic diversity. As had been the case under Manchu rule, the Chinese government—its professed dedication to equality notwithstanding—supports a de facto hierarchy of ethnic groups, with the Han having replaced the Manchus as the elites.

In certain respects the Manchu ethnic identity has, since the early 1900s, eroded and virtually disappeared with the loss of the language and cultural practices. But, as some scholars point out, the Manchus' assimilation also challenges the way Chinese is defined—specifically, by expanding that definition beyond the scope of the Han Chinese.

For centuries Mongol tribes have roamed the grasslands of east-central Asia. Here two modern-day Mongol girls churn butter at a camp in the Inner Mongolia Autonomous Region, located in northern China along the border with the independent Republic of Mongolia.

5

The Mongols

In green pastures where northern China borders Russia, the Mongols have kept their nomadic lifestyle for centuries. Their ferocity and nimble mobility earned them various epithets—some admiring and even elegant (such as "the Pearl in the Grassland"), others disparaging and suggestive of cruelty ("the barbarians"). There is a great disjuncture between the historical image of the Mongols as among the most ferocious conquerors the world has ever seen and their current reputation for "peacefulness" or even "sheepishness."

The Mongols ruled China for almost a century under leaders descended from the great Genghis Khan, who united the Mongol tribes and conquered vast territories in Asia. As conquerors, the Mongols' ferocious destructiveness gave them a bad reputation, especially among self-proclaimed moral-minded Han. For example, when the Mongols swept down from the north on their first invasion of China, they left more than 90 towns burned to the ground.

In ruling China, the Mongols' first problem was cultural. As nomads from the outskirts of Mongolia who had not had much earlier contact with China, the Mongols were too different in speech, dress, customs, and background to bridge the immediate cultural gap with the southern Han. Being generally illiterate and comparatively few in number, they used Uighur Turks, Arabs, and even some Europeans like Marco Polo to administer China. Their sparse education and cultural differences with the Han Chinese made it difficult for the Mongols to lay down roots in Beijing, historically the heart of Chinese governance. Ultimately they faded away in the late 1300s, and a new Han ruling dynasty emerged.

The Mongols in Modern China: History, Identity, and Politics

The creation of Inner Mongolia, where most of China's Mongols live, was the culmination of years of bargaining, dividing, and merging, and in this process the Mongols somehow found themselves without a voice to express their opinions about their green pastures. Still, despite ethnic and cultural links with the Republic of Mongolia, a country whose independence dates to the 1920s, most of the people of Inner Mongolia seem content (or at least resigned) to live as citizens of a Chinese state. At the same time, however, they want to maintain a separate and distinct ethnic and political identity within China. That the Mongols of China live right next door to the Republic of Mongolia makes the maintenance of a Mongolian identity separate from Chinese patronage an extremely sensitive topic in Beijing, and it may significantly complicate the policy of greater Chinese unity.

"Mongol" was initially the name of a tribe roaming along the Erguna

River. In the seventh century, the Mongols moved into the grasslands of western Mongolia. Since then they have called the area that includes Inner Mongolia and the Republic of Mongolia their home.

The most revered leader of the Mongols is Genghis Khan, who emerged in the 13th century to unify the dozen or so Mongol tribes. His ambition to subjugate China and parts of Central Asia earned the Mongols their historical place as conquerors. He led successful military campaigns against the Chinese Western Xia and Jin states, wreaking particular devastation in northern China. Ultimately, Genghis Khan spread his power as far east as Beijing, and as far west as Central Asia and southern Russia before his death in 1227. His successors expanded the boundaries of the Mongol Empire even further. But many scholars believe that the Mongols' inherently nomadic lifestyle made it difficult for them to consolidate their rule in conquered areas, and the Mongol Yuan dynasty was short lived by Chinese standards. In the centuries after the fall of the Yuan dynasty in 1368, the Mongols

In this painting, the Mongol ruler Genghis Khan (seated, upper right) watches as a prisoner is flogged. Genghis Khan was the greatest leader of the Mongols; by the time of his death in 1227, his armies had conquered a vast area stretching from China to the Caspian Sea. Although his descendants conquered more territory and established the largest land-based empire the world has ever seen, ultimately they were unable to consolidate their authority. In China, the Mongol Yuan dynasty lasted less than a century.

gradually faded into obscurity, at least insofar as mainstream Chinese culture was concerned.

What is now known as Inner Mongolia never had the cohesion characteristic of Outer Mongolia (now the Republic of Mongolia), which was unified by Buddhism. China's last imperial rulers, the Manchus, fragmented Inner Mongolia into various mutually exclusive communities and deliberately prevented the Mongols from developing a unified native religion that could serve as a focal point of ethnic identity for all Mongols. Nevertheless, Chinese control in Inner Mongolia was more nominal than actual until the early 20th century.

One of the first signs of Inner Mongolia's actual incorporation into China was the setting up, beginning in the 1910s, of Chinese special administrative zones on Mongol territory. Soon, the Mongols saw their autonomy and dominance over their green pastures diminish as Chinese settlers began to move into the region and push them off the most desirable land. In the late 1920s, China's ruling Nationalist government apportioned Inner Mongolian territory among three different provinces, thereby erasing from the map the existence of a distinct Inner Mongolia.

Mongolian political identity reemerged in the crossfire between the Chinese Communists and the Nationalists in the middle to late 1940s. For the Communists, Mongol support meant an ally in the north willing to fight against Nationalist penetration. Although the Chinese Communist Party supported some form of autonomy for the Mongols, it was careful not to create or promote Mongolian nationalism. In May 1947, while the civil war between the Nationalists and Communists was still in progress, the Chinese Communist Party established the Inner Mongolia Autonomous Region, whose government was granted only limited autonomy by the CCP.

After the ultimate victory of the Communists and the founding of the People's Republic of China in 1949, the Mongols tried to reassert their identity and their autonomy within China. One immediate priority was to reclaim land that had earlier been apportioned to various Chinese provinces. Ironically, it was the Mongols' very ambition to "recover" Inner Mongolian territory that resulted in closer integration with the Chinese.

The Mongols have not been able to solve the demographic imbalance within the region. From the outset, when the Inner Mongolia

A Mongol horseman tends to his herd. In Inner Mongolia, the traditional nomadic lifestyle of the Mongols has come under increasing pressure from Han Chinese immigration and the expansion of industrial centers.

Autonomous Region was founded with the support of the Chinese Communist Party, Mongol nationalism was curtailed by the Communist notion of class struggle. The Han Chinese living in Inner Mongolia were peasants. For Mongols it was difficult to see their neighbors as enemies intent on oppressing them, for the Chinese peasants themselves had long been oppressed under the Nationalist government. Therefore, the Mongol efforts to recover lost territory and dismantle the Chinese provincial administrative system did not actually result in a Mongol majority within the autonomous territory; nor did these efforts result in the expulsion of the Chinese migrants, who by 1949 numbered more than 4 million. On the contrary, the more territory the Mongols recovered, the more Han Chinese were incorporated into Inner Mongolia—and in turn, the less the Mongols could lay sole claim to the territory that they believed belonged to them.

The problem of the disappearing Mongol culture crystallized in the choice of the capital for the Inner Mongolia Autonomous Region. Hohhot, the Chinese Communist Party's choice for a capital city, was once a monastic center but by the 19th century had become a Chinese trading town. With few Mongol residents in and around the city, and with no Mongolian ethnic enclave, the Mongol administrators (who had been recruited from pastoral areas in eastern Mongolia) were dispersed in various residential units throughout the city, together with members of their work units. There, they comprised a minority. Within a few years, the children of Mongol Communist Party members lost their Mongolian language, and thus began a process of assimilation by default.

Under Mao, the Mongols quickly saw a dramatic reduction in autonomous rights. A massive influx of Chinese migrants arrived in Inner Mongolia as a result of Mao's land reforms and the rapid transfer to Inner Mongolia of large- and medium-size factories from coastal and inland China. Between 1950 and 1957,

Fast Facts: Mongols

Location: Inner Mongolia Autonomous Region, as well as Liaoning, Jilin, Heilongjiang, Xinjiang, Qinghai, Gansu, Ningxia, Hebei, Henan, Sichuan, Yunnan, and Beijing.

Population: 5.81 million.

Language: Three dialects: Inner Mongolian, Barag-Buryat, and Uirad. Mongolian script created in the early 13th century is based on ancient Uighur.

some 1.5 million Han Chinese migrated into Inner Mongolia. An additional 1.9 million Chinese arrived in the subsequent two years as a result of a massive famine. Much pastureland was claimed for agricultural production during this period, and the Mongols' nomadic lifestyle rapidly crumbled.

Politically, the most serious challenge to Mongol autonomy resided in the Inner Mongolia Autonomous Regional People's Congress, the highest organ of self-government. Requirements for the ethnic makeup of that body were ambiguous, which opened the door for the Han Chinese, and not the Mongols, to fill the top leadership posts. After two Mongols served as chairmen of the People's Congress from 1982 to 1992, Wang Qun—a Chinese and the former Party secretary for Inner Mongolia—assumed the chairmanship. Since then, the pattern has been for the Party secretary to serve concurrently as chair of the People's Congress—and the officeholders have been Han rather than Mongols.

Strangers in Their Own Homes

For the Mongols, the Communist revolution in China seemed to hold the promise of territorial autonomy, which in turn was supposed to bring about the regeneration of the Mongol people. Over the past 50 years, however, this lofty hope has been compromised by ethnic, territorial, political, and administrative considerations. Instead of forming a strong ethnic group, the Mongols have become further fragmented internally and further integrated into Chinese society in all aspects. This has been brought about not only by the growing demographic disparity between the Mongols and the Chinese but also by the intolerance of the Chinese regime to any sign of Mongol dissent. The Inner Mongolia Autonomous Region has, strangely enough, become in fact a region of Han autonomy, though the Mongol veneer will continue to serve a useful political function for some time to come.

A Mongol family poses outside their yurt (a traditional hide-covered dwelling) in the Inner Mongolia Autonomous Region. Note the stone wall and the windmill—telling signs of a more sedentary lifestyle for these descendants of famous nomads.

From 1978 to 1981, Mongol officials returned to power and controlled some of the key areas, such as the finance, planning, and education departments, of the Party and the government. But no longer. Today, Mongols look back with nostalgia on those few years. It was a period when the Mongols could make decisions without having to defer to the Chinese. There is also nostalgia for the period 1947–1966, when—despite many problems—Inner Mongolia enjoyed a fair measure of autonomy.

The more recent good times came to an end in 1981, when Inner Mongolia was rocked by a month-long strike by regional-college and middle school faculty and students. The strikers were protesting the government directive to increase the number of Chinese immigrants to the area. The strike revealed, in stark terms, the most basic cause of tension in Inner Mongolia: ethnicity. It was suppressed with severe repercussions for the Mongols. Not only were the student leaders punished, but more than 200 high-ranking Mongol officials were sacked or demoted for being sympathetic to the student demands.

More recently, some Mongols have begun to see themselves as comprising a virtual diaspora in their own homeland. As it stands, living in Inner Mongolia can no longer be thought of as synonymous with being "Mongolian."

The independent Republic of Mongolia offers some of China's Mongols a beacon of hope as a nation where they can live and reproduce as "pure" Mongols in a "pure" Mongolian cultural milieu. The normalization of relations between the Republic of Mongolia and China in 1989 unleashed an unprecedented desire on the part of Inner Mongolians to visit Mongolia. Many traveled north in search of a glimpse of pure Mongol-ness. But instead of being greeted as brothers and sisters, they were seen as a source of cultural pollution and a threat to the sovereignty of Mongolia. A frosty relationship between the two Mongol groups has ensued; each accuses the other of being non-Mongol in behavior and ethics. This has led to the immigration of many disillusioned young Mongols to Western Europe and the United States. It has also given rise to a renewed sense of nationalism (albeit among a minority of Mongols) whose objectives reach beyond autonomy within China to include full nationhood for the entire Mongol region.

Whither the Mongols?

Inner Mongolia has not seen large-scale ethnic violence in recent years, yet the Chinese state remains wary—some might say paranoid—of potential Mongol nationalist movements. Nor have Mongols become sullen pacifists, seeking solace or submerging their nationalist aspirations in religion; indeed, they have no such retreat. Unlike in Tibet or the Republic of Mongolia, in Inner Mongolia, Buddhism has not become a rallying point for identity. Inner Mongolian nationalism, in a way, has been antithetical to Buddhism, which has long been defined as alien and held responsible for reducing Mongolian military prowess. No single Buddhist church or leader has been identified with Inner Mongolian interests; rather, Buddhist leaders have historically served Manchu or Chinese interests, helping to pacify and control the Mongols.

The Mongols do not even have their own hero. Ironically, the Chinese have co-opted Genghis Khan, the former nemesis of the Han, as a Pan-Chinese hero and ancestor whose military feats brought glory to the Chinese nation. Numerous novels about Genghis Khan have been published in recent years; often they portray him as the only Chinese to defeat the Europeans. In 1999, a movie titled *Chinggis Khan* was shown in New York to celebrate the 50th anniversary of the founding of the People's Republic of China. In 2000, Chinese archaeologists announced that they had found the tomb of Genghis Khan in Xinjiang, thus sabotaging Mongolian efforts to find his tomb in Mongol territory. The following year, however, a team of Mongolian and American archaeologists unearthed a burial site about 200 miles northeast of Ulaanbaatar, capital of the Republic of Mongolia, that they believed was the great conqueror's final resting place. And in 2004, Mongolian and Japanese researchers found Genghis Khan's mausoleum east of Ulaanbaatar and declared that his grave would be nearby. (As of 2012, however, Genghis Khan's grave had not been found.)

In this odd competition, Mongols in China find themselves facing a dilemma. As a minority, they are happy to see their ancestral hero hailed, even worshiped, by the Chinese; but at the same time, the Chinese state is essentially appropriating their cultural heritage, leaving them unable to claim exclusive rights even to their national hero. By supporting Mongol claims that Genghis Khan is their specific hero, they risk accusations of treason from the Chinese state; by supporting Chinese claims, they betray their ancestral roots.

If neither Buddha nor Genghis Khan can serve as role model, savior, or national symbol for rallying Mongol identity, then who can? In the 21st century, the Mongols—more so than most of China's other main ethnic groups—face the difficult challenge of protecting and preserving their heritage. The question remains: who will shoulder that responsibility?

Tibetan monks blow trumpets during a festival at their monastery in Lhasa. Lamaism, a form of Buddhism that places great emphasis on the monastic hierarchy, has long been a foundation of Tibetan society.

6

The Tibetans

Tibet, as the term is understood in the West, is an ambiguous designation. In a political context, it often brings to mind the hopes for independence of a people presumed to be oppressed and is thus an extremely charged word. But it is also a deeply cultural word that refers to an entire territory inhabited by ethnic Tibetans and bound together not by political union but by commonalities of language, history, and cultural tradition. These two Tibets are not now, and seldom have been, geographically congruent.

Tibetan culture centers on a branch of Buddhism called Lamaism, which is headed by the Dalai Lama. Once the Tibetans' supreme temporal as well as spiritual leader, the Dalai Lama is revered as the incarnation of Avalokitesvara, the Buddha of Compassion. Tibet's capital, Lhasa, is considered both a religious shrine and the center of the Tibetan cultural world. In past times, virtually all Tibetans aspired to visit the sacred city at some point in their lives.

There are, however, subtle differences between the political Tibetans—those who reside in the geography defined as Tibet—and the ethnic Tibetans scattered in the provinces nearby, mostly to the east. Historically, the eastern Tibetan populations tended to enjoy less rigidly hierarchical social relations than did the populations of political Tibet. This perhaps explains why there was greater scope for economic enterprise among eastern Tibetan entrepreneurs. Tribal and clan affiliations formed the fundamental organizational structures in the east, whereas the division of land and people into aristocratic and monastic estates was more characteristic of the central Tibetan areas. In their expressions of self-identity, eastern Tibetans tended to portray themselves as belonging to strong and free confederations of warriors, in contrast with central Tibetans, whom they saw as being trapped in feudalism and subject to the whims of their lords.

Religion in Tibetan Life

In the seventh century, Buddhism (specifically, the theistic Mahayana branch) was introduced into Tibet. Several hundred years later, Lamaism began to develop with the assimilation of certain indigenous Tibetan beliefs and religious practices into Mahayana Buddhism.

The institutional heart of Tibetan Buddhism is the monastery. Monasticism was greatly encouraged in traditional Tibetan society. Monks, it was believed, were in an especially privileged position to avoid evil and achieve merit, and this merit accrued not simply to the monks themselves but to Tibetan society as a whole. In particular, individuals and families who most contributed to the monastic system were thought to benefit. Their support was believed to counterbalance, at least to some extent, the burden of sin they acquired in living their lives. Nomadic groups in the east often felt

This painting by Tibetan lamas depicts Padmasambhava, an Indian who traveled to Tibet in A.D. 747 at the invitation of the Tibetan king. Padmasambhava is credited with helping to popularize Buddhism in Tibet.

Finding the Dalai Lama

In Tibetan Buddhism, the Dalai Lama is believed to be a bodhisattva, a compassionate being who has chosen reincarnation over nirvana (deliverance from the cycle of birth, suffering, and death) in order to serve people. ("Dalai Lama" is a title, meaning "Ocean of Wisdom," rather than a personal name.)

After a Dalai Lama dies, important religious leaders—generally guided by signs and portents—search Tibet for his successor. The young boy who is the reincarnated Dalai Lama will demonstrate special knowledge. For example, the 14th Dalai Lama was identified at the age of two after he recognized a rosary that had belonged to the 13th Dalai Lama and correctly gave the names of the religious officials who were visiting his parents' house.

this to be a particularly urgent matter, for while Buddhism regards the slaughter of animals as wrong, this was an unavoidable aspect of the nomadic lifestyle. Though worldly life was thought to be inevitably ensnared in various evils, a family could still better itself spiritually by committing some sons to the clergy. And if those sons achieved religious distinction, the family's status in the society might also be favorably affected. These attitudes and outlooks helped sustain the monasteries and shrines that were to be found in nearly every locale.

In practical terms, the monastery fostered a concentration of cultural resources, serving as a center for education and the arts. It also absorbed surplus labor. For religious girls, nunneries also existed, though nuns appear to have been less numerous than monks, and they seldom had access to resources for more than a rudimentary education.

The religious life of Tibet embraced a wide range of ritual practices whose origins and purposes were diverse. Among them were the most important rituals of the central Tibetan state and of local Tibetan politicians, especially rituals concerned with state oracles and protective deities. Daily observances—such as the offering of the fragrant smoke of burnt juniper to the gods and spirits of the local environment—were, and continue to be, performed in virtually every Tibetan household. The motivation for these religious rituals often lies in the hopes for health, prosperity, and peace in this life, and for securing a positive course of rebirth in the next.

Education in the Tibetan areas also revolves largely around the monasteries, where monks learn to read, write, and recite Buddhist scriptures. Some of the lamas, after passing a test on their knowledge, will be given the degree of Gexi, the equivalent of a doctoral degree in theology. Others, after a period of training, will be qualified to serve as religious officials or preside over religious rites.

Tibetans' Place in Chinese History

The Tibetans first settled along the Yarlung Zangbo River in Tibet. Archaeological evidence indicates that the Tibetans occupied the land they now populate as far back as the third and fourth centuries. At the beginning of the seventh century, a ruler from the territory south of the Yarlung Zangbo, King Namri Songzan, began to unify the various Tibetan kingdoms. His son, King Songzan Gambo, reigned over the whole of Tibet and made "Losha"—today's Lhasa—the capital. Songzan Gambo designed official posts, defined military and administrative areas, created Tibetan script, formulated laws, and unified weights and measures, thus establishing the kingdom known as "Bo" (referred to as "Tubo" in Chinese historical documents).

After the Tubo regime was established, the Tibetans increased their political, economic, and cultural exchanges with the Han and other ethnic groups in China. The Kingdom of Tibet began to have frequent contacts with the Tang dynasty (618–907).

In the middle of the ninth century, Tibet's king was assassinated and a battle for succession ensued. The Kingdom of Tibet fell apart, and in the aftermath various competing regimes emerged and gradually moved toward a feudal system complete with serfdom. It was during this time that Buddhism was adapted to local circumstances, won increasing numbers of followers, and gradually turned into Lamaism, alongside of which a feudal hierarchy combining religious and political power emerged.

Until it became a part of modern-day China, Tibet was by and large a feudal society. At the bottom of the rigidly stratified social order were the majority of Tibetans, who toiled as serfs on the lands owned by a small aristocracy, usually high-ranking lamas. At the very top of the hierarchy was the Dalai Lama.

Under the system of feudal serfdom, the Tibetans' social life and customs bore marks of their historical traditions. As a rule, Tibetans go only by their given name (and not their family name), and the name generally tells the gender. As names are mostly taken from Buddhist scripture, namesakes are common; differentiations are made by adding "Senior," "Junior," or outstanding features of the person, or by mentioning the birthplace, residence, or profession before the name.

The social stratification of Tibet also manifests itself in the Tibetan language, which has three major forms of expression: the most respectful, the respectful, and the everyday speech. These three modes of speech are used to address superiors, peers, and inferiors, respectively.

The Tibet Debate

All sides agree that Tibet was independent of China until the Mongols emerged as a powerful force in Asia in the 13th century.

Tibetan leaders submitted to Genghis Khan in the year 1207, but Chinese claims over Tibet really begin with the creation of the Yuan (Mongol) dynasty in China in 1279. At that time Tibet, which was already subordinate to the Mongols, became part of the same empire that included China. Tibetans, however, do not see this as evidence that Tibet is a part of China. Rather, they contend that Tibet and China were, for a time, simply part the same vast empire the Mongols had assembled; and after all, the Chinese also regarded the Yuan dynasty as foreign rulers. Moreover, Tibetans argue that the relationship between the Mongol emperors of China and Tibet's lama rulers was that of "priest and patron," the Mongol rulers serving as patrons of Tibet in return for the spiritual guidance of Tibet's great lamas.

The period after the fall of the Mongol dynasty in 1368 is also contested. China claims that the ethnically Chinese Ming dynasty ruled Tibet during that time; Tibetans contend that while contacts between Tibetan lamas and the new Ming emperors continued, China exerted no authority over Tibet.

The conquest of China in 1644 by yet another non-Chinese confederation, the Manchus, soon led to Tibet's subordination. The Manchu Qing dynasty sent armies to Tibet four times during the 18th century and, in the process, established a loose protectorate over Tibet. It should be noted, however, that Tibet did not become an integral part of China at this time because it was not ruled by Chinese laws, language, and institutions. The Qing dynasty's Tibet policy was aimed at controlling the religious and lay leaders of Tibet and did not seek to sinicize Tibet's culture, institutions, and bureaucracy. Tibet continued to be ruled largely by Tibetan elites, using their own language and customs, but under the supervision of a commissioner sent by the Lifanyuan, the Qing government department established to oversee frontier territories.

From the apex of its power in Tibet at the end of the 18th century,

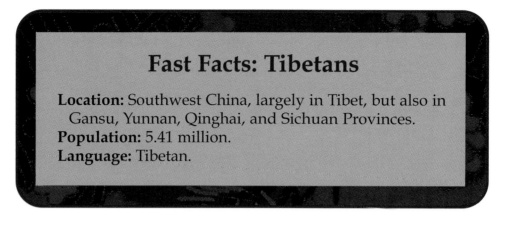

Fast Facts: Tibetans

Location: Southwest China, largely in Tibet, but also in Gansu, Yunnan, Qinghai, and Sichuan Provinces.
Population: 5.41 million.
Language: Tibetan.

the Qing dynasty's control gradually declined. In the 19th century, as the dynasty was weakened by internal disorder and external attacks by Western colonial powers, Tibet faded into the background. Seen as a backwater of little strategic interest, it received scant attention from the capital in Beijing. The Manchus continued to post imperial commissioners to, and station a military unit in, Tibet, but by the last quarter of the 19th century, Tibet paid only lip service to Chinese rule. The arrival of the British in the Himalayas changed the situation, threatening China's hegemony and stimulating a renewed Chinese interest in solidifying its position in Tibet.

During the 19th century, the British colonial government in India expanded its political influence to neighboring Nepal and made attempts to develop relations and trade with Tibet. But the Tibetan government refused to meet and discuss these issues with British officials, even after the Chinese government in Beijing asked it to do so. In 1903, fed up with years of frustration and failure, the British invaded Tibet with the aim of forcing the 13th Dalai Lama to negotiate. He refused, fleeing to Outer Mongolia when the British marched into the Tibetan capital of Lhasa.

The British invasion refocused Chinese attention on Tibet. From Beijing's vantage point, Tibet had almost been lost because the 13th Dalai Lama and his government had been ignoring Chinese instructions with impunity, so the government appointed a new

British troops in Tibet survey the landscape from a mountain outpost. This drawing was originally published shortly after the British invasion of Tibet in 1903.

imperial commissioner to take a hard-line policy that sought greater central control over Tibet.

After the fall of the Qing dynasty, China's Nationalist government set up a commission for Tibetan and Mongolian affairs. The government also established Qinghai and, later, divided large parts of cultural Tibet among it and a handful of other provinces.

Tibet Under Mao

The founding of the People's Republic of China on October 1, 1949, began a new chapter in Chinese history, and a new chapter in Sino-Tibetan relations. Tibet's inability to reach a satisfactory settlement of its status with the pre-Communist governments of China meant that it now had to deal with a considerably stronger Chinese government. The CCP, like previous Chinese regimes, considered that Tibet had been, and should again be, a part of China. Its reasons were both nationalistic and strategic. Redressing the humiliations China had suffered at the hands of Western colonialists was a goal of all nationalistic Chinese, and keeping disparate parts of China unified under a strong central government was seen as a means to that end. One of the stars on the post-1949 Chinese flag represents Tibet; the idea of allowing such a huge area to go its own way was unpalatable, particularly since not integrating Tibet potentially presented serious national-security dangers. The anti-Chinese bent of Tibet's leaders made it likely that an independent Tibet would be pulled into the orbit of the United States, which was pursuing a Cold War strategy of containing communism. If this occurred, China's potential enemies would be sitting right at the edge of Sichuan, its largest province. From the beginning, therefore, the new government unconditionally asserted its sovereignty over Tibet. And with an army of several million battle-hardened troops, there was little doubt it could impose its views on Tibet.

The question for the new rulers of China was not whether to

incorporate Tibet but how best to do so. The early nationality policy of the Chinese Communist Party was modeled after the Soviet Union's nationality system, wherein major nationality areas were given the status of republics, with considerable autonomy—at least on paper. Theoretically they even had the right to secede from the Soviet Union. By the 1940s, however, the CCP had shifted its policy on ethnic minorities to favor what it called "autonomous regions" for minority peoples. Conceptually, these autonomous regions were less autonomous than the Soviet republics and did not, for example, have the right to secede. Nevertheless, China's political system gave minority groups living in compact communities the right to exercise authority over an autonomous region where their language could be used and their customs and culture preserved. How much cultural, religious, and political autonomy was allowed, however, differed in each region.

In the case of Tibet, Mao Zedong was willing to "liberate" Tibet militarily if necessary—meaning that the Tibetans had the choice of voluntarily returning to China or being forced to do so. Mao had decided from the start that the military option would be used only as a last resort. He understood that Tibet was very different from other minority areas because it had been operating independently for four decades and because there were no Chinese living there. Mao decided, therefore, that China should make a major effort to "liberate" Tibet peacefully—that is, with the consent of the Dalai Lama and the government of Tibet. If China could accomplish this, it could avoid the risk of turning Tibet's status into an international Cold War issue. Moreover, Tibetans themselves would come to accept the legitimacy of Tibet's being a part of China.

To facilitate this goal, Mao formulated a policy of moderation and gradualism for Tibet. Socialist reforms would be emphasized immediately, but the government of the Dalai Lama would be allowed to continue to function internally.

Mao's relatively liberal terms failed to entice the Dalai Lama or his advisers to negotiate Tibet's reunification with China. Tibet's leaders were adamantly opposed to giving up their land's de facto independence and becoming part of an atheist, Communist China.

In October 1950, Mao ordered the People's Liberation Army to invade Tibet's eastern province. The aim of this attack was not so much to conquer the region as to force the Tibetan government to negotiate "peaceful" liberation. With his military forces disorganized, and bereft of outside help, the 14th Dalai Lama sent a negotiating team to Beijing; in May 1951, the leader of the Tibetan delegation reluctantly signed an agreement for Tibet's unification with China. Five months later the Dalai Lama and Tibet's National Assembly ratified the pact, which formally recognized Chinese sovereignty over Tibet for the first time. The agreement also allowed units of the Chinese army to move into Tibet to defend the borders and establish a military base; in addition, a military government was created to ensure the execution of the agreement. Now Tibet was unquestionably an integral part of China. But it also had a unique status within the country, as the Chinese agreed not to unilaterally alter Tibet's existing political system or the established status, functions, and powers of the Dalai Lama—meaning that Tibet would continue to be ruled with its own language and traditional laws.

From the beginning, tensions arose between the Tibetans and the Chinese. For example, the Tibetan government refused to replace the flag its army carried on parade with the Chinese national flag. Key Tibetan officials covertly backed the organization of a political party to protest the Chinese presence. In 1952, violence between the Chinese army and the Tibetans was only narrowly averted after the Dalai Lama dismissed two major anti-Chinese officials. But hostility and anger toward the Chinese continued, among a large portion of the Tibetan elite as well as among many common people. In the mid-1950s, after the Chinese began imposing collectivization of

Chinese troops march over the highlands toward the Tibetan frontier, October 1950. Although the Chinese agreed to respect Tibetan autonomy, Beijing's imposition of unpopular policies ultimately led to a bloody 1959 rebellion in Lhasa.

the land in eastern Tibet, sporadic fighting broke out there.

Among the Tibetan religious and secular elite, there was no real consensus about how to deal with the Chinese so as to preserve Tibetan autonomy and institutions. The Dalai Lama himself advocated reforms to Tibet's ancient system of governance, but he was unable to quell the unrest. By 1958, the U.S. Central Intelligence Agency was providing arms to pro-independence Tibetan groups.

In March 1959, matters came to a head. In Lhasa, thousands of demonstrators took to the streets, attacked pro-Chinese Tibetan officials, and demanded independence for Tibet. After days of unrest, Chinese troops moved in and put down the uprising with considerable bloodshed. In the aftermath, thousands of Tibetans were executed or imprisoned.

Meanwhile, the Dalai Lama had fled into exile in India. From

The 14th Dalai Lama, spiritual leader of Tibet, waves to supporters. Since fleeing his homeland in 1959, the Dalai Lama has been a tireless advocate for Tibetan self-government. He received the 1989 Nobel Peace Prize for his efforts to resolve the issue through nonviolent means.

there, he renounced the agreement with China and sought support for Tibet's independence and self-determination. Despite all the effort to prevent it, the Tibet question inevitably reemerged as an international and Cold War issue.

After the uprising, the Chinese government also renounced the agreement and adopted a diametrically different policy for how it would treat Tibetans and their culture. The central government terminated the traditional Tibetan government, confiscated monastic and aristocratic estates, and closed down the majority of Tibet's several thousand monasteries. The old society was gone and a new, hard-line cultural policy installed. With Mao's insistence on collectivization and agricultural communes, Tibet became another experiment of the CCP chairman. The government quickly moved to eliminate the system of serfdom, together with the elites who ruled the system, since they would never willingly accept socialist reforms. In September 1965, the Tibet Autonomous Region was officially established.

Lingering Issues

Tibet has remained restive since the uprising of 1959. Over the years, Chinese troops have been called on to put down periodic demonstrations, sometimes with significant loss of life. Chinese authorities have also imprisoned Tibetan independence activists and "reorganized" monasteries, which they appear to view as centers of opposition.

But many Tibetans believe that other Chinese actions pose a much greater threat. Particularly since the 1990s, critics charge, China has aggressively pursued a policy of resettling ethnic Han people in Tibet. Overall, ethnic Tibetans may now constitute a minority in Tibet. In Lhasa, Tibet's capital and spiritual center, close to 50 percent of the population in the inner part of the city is Han Chinese. Visitors today note more signs in Chinese than in the native script. The majority of shops also appear to be run by Chinese who have moved from all corners of the country, enticed by the central government's economic incentives.

The immigration of Han Chinese has certainly eroded the structure of Tibetan identity, and many Tibetans charge that this is precisely what Beijing wants. It would appear that Tibetans in Tibet, as well as those agitating for independence while in exile, have an uphill fight to preserve their culture.

A young Tibetan girl walks down the steps of a building in southeastern Tibet. The Chinese characters on the sign attest to the pervasive Han influence in modern-day Tibet. Particularly since the 1990s, the Chinese government has encouraged Han Chinese entrepreneurs, bureaucrats, and skilled professionals to settle in Tibet, and ethnic Tibetans may now be a minority in their homeland.

Chinese Muslims pray at a Uighur mosque in Turpan, in the Xinjiang Uighur Autonomous Region in northwestern China. The Uighurs, numbering about 8.4 million, are one of two major Muslim groups in China.

7

The Hui and the Uighurs

Over 20 million people in China—or slightly more than 1.5 percent of the overall population—are Muslim. In recent years this group, despite its small size, has posed arguably the most vocal challenge to the cohesion of Chinese identity, calling into question the very construction of Chinese nationality, society, and ethnicity.

Even before 1949, the Muslims—along with the Mongols—dominated the CCP leadership's perception of China's non-Han inhabitants. Within the Muslim community, the Chinese government looked particularly to the Chinese-speaking Muslims—the Hui—as the main strand. This is largely because many Hui Muslims lived in and around the northern parts of China, where the Communists had their headquarters in the 1930s. This familiarity ensured that the Chinese-speaking Muslims and the Mongols would occupy prominent places in the CCP's ethnic policies after the Communists came to power in 1949.

Initially, the CCP regarded the Mongols and the Hui as similar in certain fundamental respects, yet these two groups would present the Communists with very different problems of definition and governance. The Mongols in the north lived almost exclusively in their own historic and well-defined territory. They also primarily used their own language, practiced nomadic pastoralism in contrast to agriculture, and possessed a relatively homogeneous culture marked by common folkways such as food, music, horsemanship, and wrestling.

The Hui may have looked similarly well defined geographically, situated in Yan'an and its rather limited hinterland in the northern part of China. But soon after the Communist Party took power nationally, its ethnicity experts discovered that the widely distributed, culturally diverse Chinese-speaking Muslims resembled the Mongols hardly at all. Indeed, the presence of considerable numbers of Muslims throughout the Chinese cultural area has created difficulties of both perception and policy for every Chinese-based state since the beginning of the Ming dynasty in the 14th century.

Living in every province and almost every county of China, the Hui have managed simultaneously to acculturate to local society wherever they live and to remain effectively different from their non-Muslim neighbors. Most of them use the local Chinese dialect exclusively, and they have developed their customs and habits in constant interaction with local non-Muslims, whom they usually resemble strongly in their material life. Intermarriage has made them physically similar to their neighbors—with some exceptions in northwest China—but their Islamic practice and collective memory of a separate tradition and history set them apart. In short, they are both Chinese and Muslim.

The Hui are not China's only Muslim group, however, and their adaptability to Chinese culture has drawn criticism from others who follow Islam, particularly the Turkic-speaking Uighurs. Many Uighurs advocate some form of secession from the Chinese state, and some vow to use violent means to attain that goal.

In contrast to the Hui, the Uighurs are a Turkic people who came originally from the Altai Mountain region north of western Mongolia. After ruling Mongolia from the early eighth to the mid-ninth centuries, they migrated to East Turkestan, now known as Xinjiang, a province in northwest China. They have been the predominant ethnic group of the region ever since. The Uighurs,

Hui men chat on a street in Turpan, in the Xinjiang Uighur Autonomous Region. For the most part, the Hui have adapted to Chinese culture while maintaining their Muslim beliefs.

however, are not a unified people; as in the past, many continue to identify primarily with their oasis cities.

The Uighurs and Hui both follow the Sunni branch of Islam, but the commonalities largely stop there. There is considerable tension between the two groups, and much of it arises from economic competition. As some scholars have noted, the Han Chinese seem to encourage this tension because it helps prevent a cohesive Muslim identity, which might threaten Chinese control in parts of northwestern China. Yet nationalism also plays an important role in divisions between the Uighurs and the Hui. While Uighur separatists have been waging a

A man rides his bicycle past the ruined walls of Gaochang. Founded in the second century B.C., the city was the capital of an ancient Uighur kingdom. In recent years this kingdom has become a symbol for Uighur separatists advocating for the creation of an independent state, East Turkestan.

violent campaign for an independent state (which Beijing links to international Islamic terrorism), the Hui do not appear to share these aspirations for a homeland. Indeed, they seem to have more in common with the Han Chinese than with their Uighur co-religionists, which, some scholars assert, may be the result of decades of Chinese indoctrination.

Muslims in Qing China

For centuries, *Hui* was simply the Chinese word for all Muslims. The Qing dynasty basically lumped all followers of Islam, Chinese-speaking and Turkic-speaking, in the same group. Not only was there no name for what is now defined as the Hui identity, but there were few institutional connections among the Muslim communities scattered all over China (except for trading networks, which allowed Muslim merchants to find a mosque for prayer and ritually pure food as they traveled, as well as teacher-disciple networks of religious professionals). The Manchus tried to keep the Muslim community dispersed. The government had a powerful interest in discouraging widespread, unofficial organizations inside its frontiers, and voluntary associations of all kinds had long been suspect within the Chinese cultural nexus. In the view of many Qing officials, Islam, with its sacred texts and mosque-based community structure, required careful watching.

But there was no real national organization to which all Chinese-speaking Muslims might turn for redress of grievances or influence at the Qing court; nor did followers of Islam in China possess a sense of unity based on their common faith. Quite the contrary, Muslims remained regionally focused and pitted primarily against one another rather than against the Qing.

The Hui Under the Chinese Communists

The pre-1949 relationship between the northwestern Muslims and the Chinese Communists followed no single path. On the one hand,

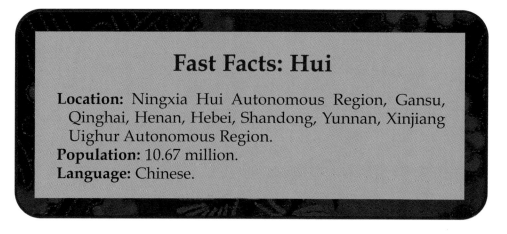

Fast Facts: Hui

Location: Ningxia Hui Autonomous Region, Gansu, Qinghai, Henan, Hebei, Shandong, Yunnan, Xinjiang Uighur Autonomous Region.
Population: 10.67 million.
Language: Chinese.

some Muslim intellectuals gave their allegiance to the Chinese Communist Party; on the other hand, the Communists encountered ferocious Muslim military resistance.

The members of the Hui, as currently defined, have no common language, no common territory, and no common economic life, though they are widely held to be naturally skillful at doing business in the marketplace. As for psychological makeup, or culture, Islam itself constitutes their sole common heritage, and their customs tend to differ from region to region, except for those that derive from their religion.

Since China's "ethnic classification" of the 1950s, and especially since 1978, communication and transportation have improved throughout the country, and the state's designation of the Hui as a coherent social entity now has considerably more validity than it ever did. Because the state has been willing to fund all kinds of official ethnicity-based institutions, members of the Hui are now aware of having a distinct ethnic identity (which many may not have been in 1949) with, for example, distinct costumes, folksongs, and literature. There are Hui research institutes, Hui exhibits at ethnicity theme parks all over China (as well as in Hawaii and Florida), and Hui variety performances on television during New Year's Eve. After years of indoctrination, many Hui are entirely convinced of the common blood they share with all other Hui.

Both Chinese and Muslim, the Hui may be seen as occupying the cultural margin of Chinese civilization, part inside and part outside. More literally, many Hui communities are physically located on the edges of the Chinese cultural area, where it abuts Southeast Asia, Tibet, Central Asia, and Mongolia. In these locations, the Hui serve as intermediaries between Chinese and non-Chinese cultures. They are not alone, for members of other ethnic and cultural groups can also perform these functions, but the Hui have proved themselves uniquely suited to the position. For example, Hui families all over China have taken up transporting, carving, and selling jade as their specialty. Even in Beijing and Shanghai, some of the most famous and prosperous jade dealers are Hui. They have undertaken this work partly because the most important domestic source for jade within China is in Xinjiang, China's huge northwestern-most province, whose population was overwhelmingly Turkic-speaking and Muslim until the mid-20th century.

The Hui's Oasis Brothers

In Xinjiang, the Hui have played an important intermediary role between the Uighurs and the Han. The Uighurs, who made their homes in the oases in what is otherwise a barren and desolate region, were perhaps Xinjiang's original settlers. The modern definition of the Uighur people as encompassing all the oasis Turks of Xinjiang hides two traditional divisions in Uighur society that have existed since A.D. 840: the strong local oasis identities, and the different strategies each oasis employs in response to political, social, economic, and geographical forces. Historically, cross-border contacts with other countries were much more frequent and important than contacts among the oases themselves.

The historical legacy of isolation among the oasis communities carries over into contemporary local conceptions of Uighur identity. Not only do Uighurs continue to identify themselves by the oasis in which they live, but perceived differences among the oases are extremely significant, influencing how Uighur intellectual elites select local heroes and manipulate Uighur history. Through this process, contesting versions of Uighur national identity are created, and those versions are accepted, rejected, or abandoned at the individual level of the peasants.

Communist China's incorporation of Xinjiang was an attempt to override the region's historical and geographical divisions. Unifying the region into an internal colony, the central government hoped, would make it easy to manage. Until 1949, Xinjiang had been relatively independent of China's central authorities and had instead been influenced by the civilizations on its western border. In cutting Xinjiang's cross-border contacts, the Communist government for the first time isolated the Uighurs from their historical, religious, kinship, and economic ties, and the imposed internal focus became a crucial factor in the development of modern Uighur identity.

Hui imams, or religious leaders, stand outside the Niu Jie Mosque in Beijing. The Hui have traditionally played an intermediary role between the Uighurs and the Han Chinese.

Soon after assuming power in China, the Communists had concluded that they could no longer afford to allow Xinjiang to

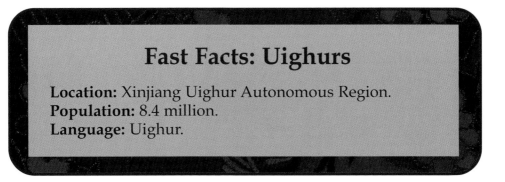

Fast Facts: Uighurs

Location: Xinjiang Uighur Autonomous Region.
Population: 8.4 million.
Language: Uighur.

govern itself with loose central supervision. The borders of Xinjiang were of major importance to Chinese security interests in relation to the Soviet Union. Furthermore, China needed the region's oil, coal, and other mineral wealth. But the increased central control created resentment among the Uighurs, as it did with the Mongols and the Tibetans.

Uighur resentment manifested itself most clearly through the vehicle of Islam, the practice of which constitutes a strongly symbolic means of confronting the Chinese state. By embracing Islam, Uighurs reject the atheism of Chinese communism as well as its goals of modernization and social liberation. In Xinjiang, Islam permeates all realms of Uighur life—political, social, and economic. In fact, the term *Muslim* as used in the region refers not only to a religious person but also to all native Central Asians. To call oneself a Uighur is to accept Islam. Even Uighur intellectuals who oppose Islamic traditionalism and its resurgence consider themselves Muslim and take part in Islamic cultural practices, demonstrating a clear symbiosis between national and religious identity.

On the surface the formation, in 1955, of the Uighur Autonomous Region in Xinjiang appeared to imply that the Uighurs would receive more power and control over their own lands. As in other autonomous regions, however, it actually meant that the central government could assert more control over the group.

Since 1979, resentment of the Han by the Uighurs has festered,

Uighurs dance during a traditional festival. Culturally, more Uighurs identify with their Turkic-speaking neighbors in Central Asia than with the Chinese.

periodically triggering riots, demonstrations, bombings, assassinations, and other forms of social and political unrest. Bombings and assassinations of pro-Beijing officials occurred in 1990, 1992, and 1997. Demonstrations and riots indicative of broader-based discontent, largely sparked by student protests, frequently centered on Uighur objections to the deportation of Han prisoners to Xinjiang and large-scale immigration into Xinjiang from eastern China. The protests reflected Uighurs' fears that the government was seeking to render them a minority in their own autonomous region by allowing the influx of Han Chinese from China Proper.

In recent years, violence between the Uighurs and the Chinese government has escalated. In 1997 the police fired on a crowd of more than 1,000 Uighur students brandishing blue East Turkestan Republic flags and seeking an end to China's rule in Xinjiang. As many as 31 protesters were killed, and nearly 200 were wounded. Following these riots, more than 10 anti-Chinese demonstrations took place in Xinjiang, one involving in excess of 5,000 Uighurs. Uighur separatists also staged violent acts, including the derailing of a train filled primarily with ethnic Han people traveling to Urumchi, the capital of Xinjiang, and the bombing of three Urumchi buses to coincide with the state funeral for Chinese leader Deng Xiaoping. Some 23 people were killed and 74 injured in these incidents. Ten days later, in Beijing, Uighur separatists exploded a pipe bomb on a bus in the Chinese capital's busiest shopping district.

Some Uighur intellectuals point out that Uighur absorption into the Chinese state is as much a form of colonization as was British control of Hong Kong. These people want an independent East Turkestan nation within territorially defined borders. In the wake of the September 11, 2001, terrorist attacks on New York City and Washington, D.C., however, China launched its own "war on terror" against Uighur separatists in Xinjiang. In this undertaking, Chinese authorities appeared to equate Islamic terrorists with the Uighur ethnicity as a whole.

But the efforts of the central government to quell Uighur unrest met with mixed results at best. Uighur grievances—political as well as economic—simmered for years before exploding in deadly violence in July 2009. The flashpoint, ironically, was an event that occurred not in Xinjiang but in the eastern province of Guangdong. At a toy factory there, ethnic Han workers attacked Uighur workers, killing two. On July 5, a relatively small number of Uighurs gathered in Urumqi to protest the killings. When police broke up the peaceful demonstration, thousands of Uighurs poured into the streets, destroying cars and stores and attacking ethnic Han. Han mobs struck back. Eventually, 20,000 Chinese troops were dispatched to Urumqi to end the rioting. About 1,600 people were wounded and 197 killed in the violence, according to official government figures. Uighur leaders, however, insisted that the actual death toll was considerably higher.

Predictably, Chinese officials downplayed widespread anger in the Uighur community as a cause of the unrest. Rather, the government blamed a small group of extremists for fomenting the violence, going so far as to say that Uighur separatists were directed by foreign Islamic terrorist organizations like al-Qaeda. This focus on terrorism has, for the time being at least, foreclosed the possibility of a dialogue to address the legitimate concerns of the Uighur people.

A Miao woman wears a huge silver headdress at a Lunar New Year festival in Kaili, a town in China's southwest Guizhou Province. Officially China's fourth-largest minority group, the Miao—who are related to peoples in Vietnam, Laos, Thailand, and Burma—remain somewhat difficult to classify with precision.

The Miao and the Yao

The Miao and the Yao, peasants and herders of China's interior, have conventionally been known for their "remoteness"—for being isolated in inaccessible and forbidding territory. Among the Han Chinese, this notion of remote peoples carries a double significance. On the one hand, it conjures up romantic images of a pristine landscape shrouded in mystical beauty. On the other hand, it represents a judgment about the marginalized and uncivilized, of economic and social malaise, of dispossessed people living in deep poverty, scratching out a living in the most infertile of China's hill country.

For many centuries of Chinese history, the territory of the southwest has been a ground of political struggle and competition for scarce resources. Southwestern China was the frontier, an unevenly governed area that marked the outer reaches of empire, a place where borders, taxes, and subjection were regularly contested. This is the land that the Miao and Yao people call home, a land where for centuries they have scratched out a difficult and precarious existence. Migration to bordering Southeast Asian states has created an overseas diaspora of Miao and Yao people. The often tenuous border relations between China and Southeast Asian countries such as Thailand, Vietnam, and Laos also makes the Miao and Yao people's status highly politicized, and the complexity of their relationships with each other and with the peoples of neighboring states complicates the efforts of scholars and the Chinese government to identify and label them in distinct categories.

The Miao

The people placed in the Miao category by the CCP's ethnicity experts are counted as members of China's fourth-largest minority group. This aggregate has significant numbers (8.94 million in 2000), measurable political recognition, and high visibility in popular culture. But who are the Miao really?

Attempts to define them with objective characteristics are frustrating at best. Scattered over seven provinces, with the densest concentrations in Guizhou, Yunnan, and Hunan, the people called the Miao are speakers of several mutually unintelligible dialects and have little contact with one another across regions. Primarily agriculturalists, they grow either wet or dry rice, maize, potatoes, buckwheat, or other grains, depending on the region they inhabit. Some of them have long settled in river valleys, while others are semi-nomadic, using swidden farming on mountain slopes. Beyond China's borders, they have migrated into Vietnam, Laos, Thailand, and Burma. There, they refer to themselves as Hmong, one of the many labels used among the Miao in China.

In many respects, the fourth-largest minority group recognized by China seems more a construct of the state than a deeply rooted ethnic identification. According to Chinese government statistics, 2.68 million Miao were counted in 1965; by 1978, that number had jumped to 3.98 million. And with the comprehensive census of 1982, a total of 5 million people identified themselves as Miao. Even allowing for lenient implementation of family-planning policies, these numbers cannot be explained by an increase in reproductive rates alone; significant numbers of people previously identified as Han must have reclassified themselves as Miao.

Origins of the Miao Identity

As early as the Qin and Han dynasties more than 2,000 years ago, the ancestors of the Miao people roamed the western part of present-day Hunan Province and the eastern part of present-day Guizhou Province. In the third century A.D., the ancestors of the Miao migrated west to present-day northwest Guizhou and southern Sichuan Province along the Wujiang River. In the fifth century, some Miao people moved to eastern Sichuan and western Guizhou. By the Tang dynasty (618–907), official documents referred to the Miao as a distinct group. In the ninth century, some Miao were taken to Yunnan as captives; in the 16th century, another group settled on Hainan Island. And today the Miao diaspora extends beyond China's borders into Southeast Asia.

The Miao people's large-scale migrations over the course of many centuries have made the population widely dispersed, with each subgroup developing differences in dialect, names, and clothes, among other cultural features. Miao people from different areas often have great difficulty communicating with one another. Their art and festivals also differ from region to region.

Despite these and other significant differences among subgroups, some generalizations about the Miao can be made. By all historical accounts, the Miao everywhere were agriculturalists; they were often tenants and rarely landlords (except in southeast Guizhou,

The Miao are primarily farmers. This Miao agricultural village is located in Guizhou Province.

where they were more prosperous and more class-differentiated). They typically lived in small villages, averaging 10 to 20 households, on mountain slopes remote from centers of Han settlement. Miao society was predominantly patriarchal. Their religion combined animism, ancestor worship, and shamanism, and animal sacrifices were a key part of their rituals.

Struggle Against Oppression

Throughout their history, the Miao have taken up arms to fight against oppressive rulers. In 1795, for example, a group of Miao oppositionists led an insurrection in west Hunan and northeast Guizhou against the Qing. A huge rebel force swept across a vast area, dealing corrupt Han and Manchu officials and local tyrants a crushing blow.

Since its early years, the Chinese Communist Party has paid a great deal of attention to the "liberation" of ethnic minorities. In December 1926, a draft resolution concerning the liberation of the Miao and Yao peoples was adopted at the first peasant representative assembly in Hunan. When Mao's army passed through Miao areas during the Long March in December 1934, the army was told to respect the customs and habits of minority peoples. Many Miao people, convinced of the Chinese Communists' dedication to protecting ethnic minorities, decided to join Mao's army. Miao volunteers fought with the Communists during the civil war against the Nationalists; they also helped the Communists suppress bandits who had been rampant in western Hunan.

From the autumn of 1950 to the spring of 1951, the Chinese government led a campaign to redistribute farmland and dismantle the feudal system of land tenancy in southwestern China. But in the area where the Miao population was densest, in Guizhou, land redistribution came at a slower pace. And even as the country

Fast Facts: Miao

Location: Guizhou, Yunnan, Hunan, Sichuan, and Guangxi Zhuang Autonomous Region; also on Hainan Island and Hubei Province.

Population: 8.94 million.

Language: The Miao language belongs to the Miao-Yao branch of the Chinese-Tibetan language family. It has three main dialects in China—one based in west Hunan, one in east Guizhou, and the other in Sichuan, Yunnan, and part of Guizhou. In some places, people who call themselves Miao use the languages of other ethnic groups.

embarked on an effort to industrialize under Mao's leadership, the Miao continued to eke out a meager livelihood growing grain on mountain terraces; most lived on the edge of hunger in roadless villages without electricity.

In the post-Mao era, the Chinese government under Deng Xiaoping abandoned Mao's program of collective agriculture and restored household farming, which was second nature to the Miao. At the same time, however, Deng was pursuing a new economic policy designed to integrate China into the global economy. This meant opening up China's long-closed doors to foreign capital, speeding up the industrialization of its cities, and moving from a state-controlled economy toward a system that increasingly relied on private enterprise. One early result was soaring inflation, and Miao peasants, facing an ever-widening gap between their meager cash flow as household farmers and the fast-paced, big-money privatized national economy, felt the squeeze.

For the vast majority of Miao peasants, Deng's admonition to get rich through private ventures (and thereby advance China's modernization) was unrealistic and unattainable: they lacked the resources for start-up; their regions were relatively inaccessible by major transportation networks, making export difficult if not impossible; and the land was only suitable for a handful of cash crops, such as fruit, tea, or tobacco. The special economic zones created under Deng along the eastern coast of China courted foreign investors with tax breaks, reduction of red tape, and other incentives, leaving other areas to vie for foreign funds at a sharp disadvantage. Moreover, Guizhou and Hubei, the inland regions that are home to a large number of Miao, were too isolated to naturally attract foreign capital. Whereas the provinces along the coast received 92 percent of the total foreign capital, Guizhou took in a mere 0.22 percent.

The Yao

Like the Miao, the Yao are known as mountain-dwellers, and they are also dispersed throughout a number of southern and south-western Chinese regions. Many Yao communities were isolated from the rest of the country, making the Yao experience of poverty not entirely dissimilar from that of the Miao.

And as with the Miao, historically there has been much contention over how to define the Yao identity. After all, the Yao living in different parts of the country possessed more than 30 names for themselves, and more than 300 different terms for Yao exist in the Chinese language. (Most are descriptive of clothing or styles of ornamentation.) Only half of the Yao actually speak the Yao language, which belongs to the Chinese-Tibetan language family; the others use Miao or Dong languages. And because of close contacts with the Han and Zhuang peoples, many Yao can also speak Chinese or Zhuang.

The name Yao was officially adopted after the founding of the People's Republic of China in 1949, and territorial location ultimately became the determining factor in the government's designation of Yao ethnic identity. The Yao, the CCP asserted, were

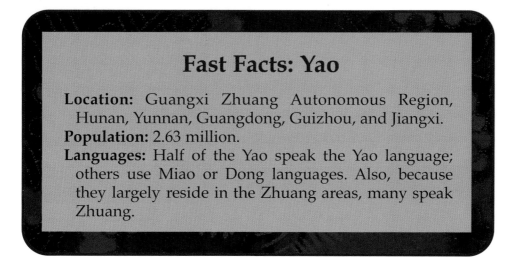

Fast Facts: Yao

Location: Guangxi Zhuang Autonomous Region, Hunan, Yunnan, Guangdong, Guizhou, and Jiangxi.
Population: 2.63 million.
Languages: Half of the Yao speak the Yao language; others use Miao or Dong languages. Also, because they largely reside in the Zhuang areas, many speak Zhuang.

those who lived in the remote mountain ranges in Guangdong, Guangxi, Hunan, and southern Yunnan. Long ago, Han settlers in search of new arable land had forced the Yao into these isolated territories, where they took to swidden cultivation, roamed the southern highlands, and practiced an esoteric form of Taoism (which originally developed among the Han Chinese). The widespread Yao adherence to Taoist practice is perhaps the single

Historically, the Yao lived in impoverished and isolated villages located in rugged mountain regions. This photo shows a Yao village in the Guangxi Zhuang Autonomous Region.

distinctive characteristic that differentiates them from other upland peoples, such as the Miao.

Tracing Yao Identity

About 2,000 years ago, the ancestors of today's Yao people lived around Changsha, capital of present-day Hunan Province, and were referred to by the Han as the "savage Wuling tribes." Later, they acquired the name "Moyao," and reference is made to them in a verse by Du Fu (712–770), one of China's most famous poets: "The Moyaos shoot wild geese; with bows made from mulberry trees."

In later centuries, the Yao—as they came to be called—appeared more frequently in Han historical accounts, indicating growing ties between the two peoples. During the Song dynasty (960–1279), the Yao were renowned for making such products as forged-iron knives and indigo-dyed cloth; in Hunan at this time, they are known to have raised cattle and cultivated fields rented from Han landlords. Later, during the Ming (1368–1644) and Qing (1644–1911) dynasties, the Yao in Guangxi and Guangdong took to raising cattle; they also developed paddy fields and planted various crops on hillsides, supplementing their agricultural pursuits with sideline occupations such as hunting, collecting medical herbs, making charcoal, and weaving. Among the Yao in certain areas, forestry was also an important source of income.

The Political Place of the Yao

Beginning around A.D. 1000, the Yao were ruled mostly by hereditary headmen, who in turn obeyed whichever dynasty happened to be reigning in China at the time. At various points, however, the Yao rebelled against the authority of the central government. Between 1316 and 1331, for example, they launched more than 40 uprisings against the Mongol Yuan dynasty. Ming dynasty rulers faced a century-long Yao revolt that began in 1371. Ultimately the Ming emperors dispatched three huge armies to subdue the rebels.

These Yao girls live in Guangxi, which has autonomous Yao communities in the counties of Bama and Jinxui.

Still later, in the 1850s, many Yao people fought against the Manchu Qing dynasty in the famous Taiping Rebellion.

In the second decade of the 20th century, after the collapse of the Qing dynasty, the Nationalists took power in China. In order to control the often-restive Yao, they governed through puppet head-men and frequently incited conflicts between the various Yao communities, pursuing a policy of "divide and rule."

After coming to power in 1949, China's Communist government officially recognized the Yao people as an ethnic minority and created various autonomous counties for them, including the Yao Autonomous County of Bama and Jinxui Yao Autonomous County, both in Guangxi. As with other ethnic minorities, the Chinese government presented the creation of these autonomous areas as a means of empowering the Yao and a mode of democratic local self-rule. But it also provided a clear opportunity for the CCP to reconstruct and formalize a state-approved definition of what it means to be a Yao.

Tibetan protesters in New York City urge the United Nations to address China's policies in their homeland, April 2004. Since the 1950s, Tibetans have campaigned for independence from China, garnering significant international attention. In recent years, independence movements have emerged among Mongols and Uighurs as well.

China's Policy Toward Ethnic Unity

How might the nationality and ethnicity policy of China be summed up? Since the Chinese Communist Party took power, the first and most important factor in the policy was the recognition—for the first time in Chinese history—of the various ethnic groups as independent nationalities. Both the early 1950s and the late 1980s saw some basic steps taken to give equal legal status and rights to all nationalities. New written languages have been created for a number of minorities who had none previously. In many regions, an industrial base has been created and educational and health care institutions established.

Class Struggles

But since the end of the 1950s, progress has been impeded in most regions—both minority and Han—

largely because of misguided political policies for which the Chinese Communist Party bears responsibility. While the CCP happily accepted minority identities at the start, its edict of a class struggle ultimately eroded the cohesion of many ethnic groups and inhibited the preservation of their identity. In periods of political campaigns, particularly the Great Leap Forward (1958–1960) and the Cultural Revolution (1966–1976), ethnic distinctions were often sacrificed and attempts were made to assimilate ethnic minorities forcibly into Han Chinese culture.

Mao strongly believed that identity could be defined by unifying behind the idea of class struggle. Tensions along ethnic lines, Mao believed, were in essence a problem of class. According to this analysis, nationality and ethnic lines would naturally disappear when class differences disappeared. What emerged would be a homogeneous working-class culture. While the element of class struggle in China can largely be traced to Mao, the drive for uniformity runs throughout centuries of Chinese history and was embraced by ruler after ruler. All pushed to tame and assimilate those who lived differently from them, either forcibly or through gentle coercion.

Under Mao, all regions and ethnic identities suffered the consequences of the political campaigns, with their disastrous mistakes in economic and social policy. But there was one crucial difference in the effects of Mao's ideology of class struggle on the Han and the minorities. The ethnic minorities considered the policies of the Communist Party, which had resulted in oppression, discrimination, and coercive action, to be national oppression by the Han and "their party." The Han Chinese, on the other hand, placed the blame on the Communist Party or a faction of the Party leadership. The political mistakes of the CCP in national minority regions were doubly grave because they led to, or reinforced, national contradictions and conflicts. All the old resentments against the Han were revived and national resistance intensified.

Continuing Challenges

Rooting out minority mistrust of the Han has been and will be a long and difficult process. Such mistrust, which has evolved over the course of history, has received new sustenance from political movements of the last few decades. When the CCP came into power in 1949, it brought some hope for the minorities. The Soviet model of giving autonomy to its republics led the Chinese minorities to believe that perhaps they would receive the same treatment under Chinese communism. In fact, many ethnic minorities fought side by side with the CCP during the civil war against the Nationalists. But the hopes were largely dashed when the Chinese Communists invaded Tibet and made it clear that Inner Mongolia would remain a part of China. The CCP has tried over the years to reestablish a basis of trust through economic policies and by granting broader autonomy in some spheres. The economic policy implemented in the early 1980s, and accompanying improvements in material living conditions throughout the country, did, to some extent, restore the Party's prestige.

At first, clear demands for independence from China existed only in Tibet, if for no other reason than that elsewhere the ethnicities were dispersed across regions and did not have the means to unite for secession. But, as discussed in earlier chapters, significant numbers of Xinjiang's Uighurs and Inner Mongolia's Mongols are now agitating to separate. An official report lists at least a dozen separatist organizations in Xinjiang. They all call themselves "Turkic" movements and have connections to Pan-Turkic organizations in nearby Central Asian countries as well as Turkey. One Chinese Communist Party official for Xinjiang once said that these separatist tendencies were the "greatest danger for Xinjiang."

Individual movements for independence do not necessarily pose any serious threat to the state, but there is a real risk that discontent could multiply over the long term if minority demands for economic and cultural development and for more autonomy are not met. Although the Chinese government has been attempting to find the right formula, in recent years, there have been signs of a hardening of its policies on minorities, primarily in Tibet and Xinjiang. Particularly since September 11, 2001, the Chinese government has implied that rumblings for independence among its Muslim population in the northwest should be seen in the context of international Islamic terrorism. In its attempts to quash dissent among the Uighurs, the Tibetans, and others, the government has shown that it sees the demands for secession as a growing threat to its power and to the unity of the nation. National security is also a concern, particularly in the border regions where China's ethnic minority groups

Two Chinese men view an exhibit on the East Turkestan Islamic Movement, Hotan, Xinjiang Uighur Autonomous Region. Since the September 11, 2001, attacks on the United States, Chinese leaders have attempted to frame the issue of Uighur separatism as part of the problem of international Islamic terrorism.

have cultural ties with minority groups in neighboring countries, such as Kazakhstan, Kyrgyzstan, Russia, North Korea, Mongolia, Thailand, and Burma.

There are essentially two main factors that undermine the national and cultural identity of minorities in China. First, lower-level Communist Party officials often obstruct the implementation of the Party's own pro-ethnic policies. They continually interfere, in ways trivial and profound, in the lives of the minorities, thereby creating tensions between the Han and the "others."

The second factor is "Pan-Han chauvinism," which finds expression in insensitivity toward, and even contempt for, the habits, customs, and cultures of the minorities. From the central government to the local level, the bureaucracy has been unable or unwilling to promote modernization and development on the one hand while also deferring to the customs and cultural identity of the ethnic groups on the other. The opening up of minority regions and their settlement by Han Chinese in disregard of ethnic cultural ways has produced a substantial backlash. While the 1982 constitution and the law of autonomy of 1984 formally proclaimed wide-ranging rights, the realization of equality and greater autonomy for China's ethnic minorities remains a long way off. Local minorities still do not enjoy true self-administration or self-determination in matters of economic and cultural development, and they have practically no influence on Han migration into their areas.

Over time that migration, combined with demographic factors, may contribute to increasing tensions between China's minorities and its dominant majority. Thus far, the impact of Han migrants in minority regions has been blunted to some degree by social separation; in many areas interaction between Han and minority populations is minimal. But that situation can continue only as long as space and resources permit. Some of the minority groups, being exempt from the official pressures for birth control, have rapidly growing populations. At the same time, large numbers of Han people have been moving to the countryside each year. It is highly likely that the needs and expectations of the Han migrants will come into conflict with those of the growing indigenous populations.

But the problem is not likely to be confined to that of competition for scarce material resources. The present, rather low level of education of most minorities allows Han settlers to occupy positions as teachers, doctors, skilled workers, and administrators without serious challenge from minorities. Recognizing the gravity of this situation, the government has introduced programs to increase the educational and employment opportunities open to minorities. Yet if these programs succeed, they will certainly throw members of the indigenous population into competition with Han settlers.

To deflect calls for independence or true autonomy in regions such as Tibet and Xinjiang, the Chinese government has invested heavily in infrastructure projects, building roads and railroads linking these remote areas with the rest of China. The government has also, at least on paper, committed itself to an affirmative-action policy that offers special advantages to minority people in education, the economy, and government.

China has also used trade to undermine foreign support of nationalist causes within its borders. Increased Chinese investment in, and trade with, its Central Asian neighbors has limited their support for Uighurs seeking independence in Xinjiang. The government has employed a similar strategy to head off Pan-Mongol aspirations in the Inner Mongolia Autonomous Region, reviving China's political and economic ties with the Republic of Mongolia.

The call for an independent Tibet, which continues to resonate internationally, has presented the longest-lasting challenge to China's attempts to maintain some uniformity within a multiethnic state. Placed on the defensive, Chinese leaders have formulated a Tibet policy that, since the 1990s, has largely relied on greater

Uighur students listen to their teacher during class in Korla, Xinjiang Uighur Autonomous Region. In 2004, the government of China embarked on a campaign to improve Chinese language skills among teachers in Xinjiang, hoping that would help assimilate Muslims into Han Chinese culture.

investment and greater opportunities for economic development to mute dissident voices.

A successful economic policy, including rising living standards, may also blunt other resentments. But reconciling the competing claims of the Han and the minorities will always constitute a delicate balancing act. In the near future at least, many minority groups will continue to lag far behind the Han economically. And if they choose to take up the wider opportunities offered to them, minorities will inevitably have to participate more deeply in the Han political and cultural order. The price of that participation may ultimately turn out to be a loss of their ethnic identities.

Glossary

assimilation—the process by which a minority group adopts the culture, language, and social conventions of the majority.

autonomous region—an area in China where there is typically a high population of a particular ethnic group and a specific administrative government formed to cater to the cultural and economic needs of that group (for example, the Xinjiang Uighur Autonomous Region and Guangxi Zhuang Autonomous Region).

autonomy—the state of being self-governing; the right to self-government.

cadre—an indoctrinated and usually highly motivated member of the Communist Party.

Confucianism—an ethical system—emphasizing humanity, the value of learning, devotion to the family (including ancestors), and peace and justice—that was taught by the philosopher Confucius and his disciples and that forms an important basis of Chinese public and private morality.

diaspora—the dispersion of a people from their original homeland; the group of people living away from the ancestral homeland.

dissident—one who disagrees with an established political system.

dynasty—a race or succession of rulers of the same line or family; the continued lordship of a race of rulers.

ethnic identity—a shared racial, national, religious, linguistic, or cultural heritage.

hegemony—domination.

lama—a monk in Lamaism, a form of Buddhism that is the predominant religion among Tibetans.

migration—the movement of a group of people from one geographical area to another.

national identity—how a group defines itself as a nation.

nomads—people who have no fixed home and move from place to place (typically seasonally) in search of food, water, and grazing land for their herd animals.

secession—the act of leaving, withdrawing, or separating from an alliance or state.

separatist movement—a typically organized, mass effort by an ethnic, racial, or religious minority to break away from a state.

sinicize—to make more Chinese.

Further Reading

Bulag, Uradyn E. *The Mongols at China's Edge: History and the Politics of National Unity.* Lanham, Md.: Rowman and Littlefield, 2002.

———. *Nationalism and Hybridity in Mongolia.* Oxford, England: Clarendon Press, 1998.

Crossley, Pamela Kyle. *The Manchus.* Oxford, England: Blackwell Publishers, 1997.

Dillon, Michael. *China's Muslim Hui Community: Migration, Settlement and Sects.* Richmond, England: Curzon, 1999.

Dreyer, June Teufel. *China's Forty Million: Minority Nationalities and National Integration in the People's Republic of China.* Cambridge, Mass.: Harvard University Press, 1976.

Eberhard, Wolfram. *China's Minorities: Yesterday and Today.* Belmont, Calif.: Wadsworth Publishing, 1982.

Elliot, Mark C. *The Manchu Way: The Eight Banners and Ethnic Identity in Late Imperial China.* Stanford, Calif.: Stanford University Press, 2001.

Gladney, Dru C. *Muslim Chinese: Ethnic Nationalism in the People's Republic.* Cambridge, Mass.: Harvard University Press, 1991.

Goldstein, Melvyn C. *A History of Modern Tibet: 1913–1951.* Berkeley: University of California Press, 1989.

Goldstein, Melvyn C.; William Siebenschuh; and P. Tsering. *The Struggle for Modern Tibet.* Armonk, N.Y.: M.E. Sharpe, 1997.

Harrell, Stevan, ed. *Cultural Encounters on China's Ethnic Frontiers.* Seattle: University of Washington Press, 1994.

Heberer, Thomas. *China and its National Minorities: Autonomy or Assimilation?* Armonk, N.Y.: M.E. Sharpe, 1989.

Kaup, Katherine Palmer. *Creating the Zhuang: Ethnic Politics in China.* Boulder, Colo.: Lynne Rienner Publishers, 2000.

Litzinger, Ralph A. *Other Chinas: The Yao and the Politics of National Belonging.* Durham, N.C.: Duke University Press, 2000.

Ma, Yin. *China's Minority Nationalities.* Beijing: Foreign Language Press, 1989.

Mackerras, Colin. *China's Minorities: Integration and Modernisation in the Twentieth Century.* Hong Kong: Oxford University Press, 1994.

———. *China's Minority Cultures: Identities and Integration Since 1912.* New York: St. Martin's Press, 1995.

Moser, Leo J. *The Chinese Mosaic: The Peoples and Provinces of China.* Boulder, Colo., and London: Westview Press, 1985.

Mullaney, Thomas. *Coming to Terms with the Nation: Ethnic Classification in Modern China.* Berkeley: University of California Press, 2010.

Rossabi, Morris, ed. *Governing China's Multiethnic Frontiers.* Seattle: University of Washington Press, 2004.

Rudelson, Justin Jon. *Oasis Identities: Uighur Nationalism Along China's Silk Road.* New York: Columbia University Press, 1997.

Schein, Louisa. *The Miao and the Feminine in China's Cultural Politics.* Durham, N.C.: Duke University Press, 2000.

Shakya, Tsering. *The Dragon in the Land of Snows: A History of Modern Tibet Since 1947.* New York: Columbia University Press, 1999.

Internet Resources

https://www.cia.gov/library/publications/the-world-fact-book/geos/ch.html

The CIA World Factbook provides a wealth of statistical and other information about China and its ethnic groups.

http://english.peopledaily.com.cn/data/minorities/ethnic_minorities.html

This site, maintained by the *People's Daily*, the official newspaper of the Chinese Communist Party, has pages for each of China's ethnic minorities.

http://www.china.org.cn/e-groups/shaoshu/index.htm

A comprehensive site on China's ethnic groups, containing information on historical, political, and economic matters.

Index

Numbers in **bold italics** refer to captions.

Picture Credits

Contributors

SHU SHIN LUH is an experienced journalist who has written on a wide range of topics. As a technology reporter for the *Washington Post*, Ms. Luh covered the beginnings of the deregulation of the U.S. telecommunications industry. She has also won awards in the United States for her reporting on consumer rights.

After returning home to Asia, where she grew up in Taiwan and Hong Kong, Ms. Luh focused her reporting largely on business strategy and economic reform in Asian countries, writing first for the *Asian Wall Street Journal*, and later freelancing for publications such as the *South China Morning Post*, the *Washington Post, American Lawyer* magazine, and *Corporate Counsel* magazine. She has closely followed China's ascension to the World Trade Organization, writing feature analysis for *American Lawyer* and *Corporate Counsel*. She is also the author of *The People of China,* another book in this series.

Ms. Luh's book *Business the Sony Way: Secrets of the World's Most Innovative Electronics Giant*, published in May 2003, has been translated into Japanese and Chinese.

Ms. Luh currently resides in London.

JIANWEI WANG, a native of Shanghai, received his B.A. and M.A. in international politics from Fudan University in Shanghai and his Ph.D. in political science from the University of Michigan. He is now the Eugene Katz Letter and Science Distinguished Professor and chair of the Department of Political Science at the University of Wisconsin–Stevens Point. He is also a guest professor at Fudan University in Shanghai and Zhongshan University in Guangzhou.

Professor Wang's teaching and research interests focus on Chinese foreign policy, Sino-American relations, Sino-Japanese relations, East Asia security affairs, UN peacekeeping operations, and American foreign policy. He has published extensively in these areas. His most recent publications include *Power of the Moment: America and the World After 9/11* (Xinhua Press, 2002), which he coauthored, and *Limited Adversaries: Post-Cold War Sino-American Mutual Images* (Oxford University Press, 2000).

Wang is the recipient of numerous awards and fellowships, including grants from the MacArthur Foundation, Social Science Research Council, and Ford Foundation. He has also been a frequent commentator on U.S.-China relations, the Taiwan issue, and Chinese politics for major news outlets.